Computer Programing

for the Complete Idiot

DONALD H. McCUNN

DESIGN ENTERPRISES OF SAN FRANCISCO

To My Wife
For Everything

Copyright©1979 by Donald H. McCunn

Library of Congress Catalog Card Number: 79-53299

International Standard Book Number: 0-932538-04-5

Printed in U.S.A

TRS-80 is a registered trademark of the Tandy Corporation.

IMPORTANT NOTICE

The author and Design Enterprises of San Francisco shall have no liability or responsiblity to any person or entity with respect to any liability, loss or damage caused or alleged to be caused directly or indirectly by the information contained in this book.

It is the user's responsibility to test any program, run and test sample sets of data, and run the program in parallel with the system previously in use for a period of time adequate to insure that the results of the operation of the program are satisfactory.

DESIGN ENTERPRISES OF SAN FRANCISCO
P.O. Box 27677
San Francisco, California, 94127

Acknowledgments

The acknowledgments for this book must start with an expression of deep gratitude to two institutions which have made the technology of micro-computers possible.

NASA, through its efforts to explore space, funded the research that was required to reduce what used to be a roomful of computer equipment into a small chip that is about the size of a thumbnail. Without this pioneering technology, computers would still only be available to large corporate giants. Now, almost anyone who wants to may have the power of the computer at their fingertips.

Dartmouth College is the institution which invented the programing language called BASIC. It is through this language that a person with very little, if any, technical background can communicate with the computer. This BASIC language provides incredibly versatile possiblities while using a minimum number of computer instructions. Without this simple, straightforward language, most people would probably not have the time or interest to learn how to run a computer.

More immediately, I would like to thank Erwin, Tom, and Betty Barth of Radio Shack's Computer Center for their kindness and consideration. I would also like to thank Dave Sparks for his technical assistance.

I am very grateful to Lynda Preston and Roxey for their careful reading of the manuscript and editorial suggestions. A special note of thanks is due Graem Atkinson for his contributions and consultations.

Table of Contents

Introduction   7

THE COMPUTER   10
  Basic Operating Procedures   11
  Basic Programing Procedures   20
  Program Storage   30

THE COMPUTER PROGRAM   33
  The Program Description   35
  Stored Information   37
  Input Information   43
  Corrections   49
  Simple Calculations   54
  Multiple Functions   57
  Information Storage   65
  Advanced Calculations   71
  The Totaling Program   87

CREATING ORIGINAL PROGRAMS   99
  Program Information   103
  Program Calculations   110
  Program Outputs   111
  Debugging Programs   118

    Appendixes   120
    Index   124
    Glossary   126

INTRODUCTION

Computer programing is the process of creating a set of instructions that tell the computer to perform a given task. With the advent of the new personal computers, this is no longer the exclusive domain of computer specialists. Now anyone may create programs which will put the incredible power of the new micro-computers at their fingertips.

People have been applying these inexpensive table-top computers to many different uses in business, education, and in the home. Individuals are creating programs both to run part-time businesses and to help make top level management decisions for some of the nation's largest corporations. Educators, aware that the future of many young people will depend on their ability to program computers (the three R's and the big P), are introducing computers into the classroom for a wide variety of applications. Other individuals are creating programs for personal financial planning and record keeping. And finally, hobbyists have only begun to explore the many potential uses of the computer.

To a large extent, the versatility of the new personal computers comes from the fact that the person who is using the computer can also create the programs that run it. This is important because every application will have its own unique differences. The person who is using the computer knows better than anyone else the exact task they want the computer to perform. Furthermore, as circumstances change, programs can be adapted to meet the needs of new situations. But most importantly, computers can open up new sources of information that only the user will recognize.

The chief value of the computer is that it can save enormous amounts of time in recording information, calculating, filing, correlating files, and recovering data. In business, for example, simple transactions, such as the sale of a product or service, result in mounds of paperwork including sales receipts, billings, invoices, statements, sales tax records, ledger entries, inventory reports, sales reports, profit and loss statements, business tax records, and income tax records. If each transaction is initially entered into the computer, all subsequent information can be automatically generated by the computer. It takes the computer a very small fraction of the time to process the data compared to the time required to do this by hand kept records. The tremendous savings in time and effort in handling these transactions means that the computer can do for paperwork what the wheel did for transportation.

Since the chief value of the computer is its ability to save time, it must not take an inordinate length of time to create original programs. This book has been designed to first introduce the reader to the basics of how computers work. It then goes on to explain how programs can be written to make computers achieve specific tasks.

It is not necessary to know all the technical details of how a computer works in order to create programs anymore than it is essential to know how an internal combustion engine works to drive a car. Therefore, technical information about computers has been omitted from the description unless it is essential to the development of programs.

This book is divided into three parts. The first part describes the basic operating and programing procedures for the new personal micro-computers. The second part describes how programs achieve a specific task and the final part describes how to create original programs.

The new micro-computers use a programing language called BASIC. This BASIC language allows people to communicate with computers using simple English words of five letters or less. While most of the various brands of micro-computers use this same language, each model has slight differences in how it responds to the language. For example, the computer tells the operator it is ready to go to work by printing a signal on a television-like screen. Some computers use the word READY for this signal, others use OK, and at least one model prints an asterisk.

This book describes the specific operation of Radio Shack's TRS-80. This model was selected because Radio Shack has many stores around the United States as well as outlets throughout the world so the TRS-80 is readily accessible. It is also the most economical model currently available. This economy comes from Radio Shack's leaving off elaborate computer features rather than from inexpensive manufacturing techniques. The convenience of the Radio Shack Stores makes it possible for the reader to try running a computer. The first two sections of the book, Basic Operating Procedures and Basic Programing Procedures, may be processed through a computer in about fifteen minutes. Read these sections carefully, take the book into a Radio Shack Store and try operating a computer. To apply the descriptions in this book to other computer models, first consult their owner's manuals to learn the specific operating procedures.

The second part of the book describes how programs may be written to achieve a given task. Programs can be developed in many different ways, but the basic process the computer follows is to take in information, manipulate it, and then display the results of the manipulation. The program format described in this book takes each separate part of the process and shows how the individual segments of a program may be developed to handle a desired task.

The program format is described using a specific example, a Payroll Program. Each individual part of the Payroll Program may be typed in and tried out as the program is being developed so that the reader may see how a computer responds. The program should be tried out on a computer as much as the reader's circumstances allow. It is very difficult to learn programing without actually using a computer just as it is difficult to learn how to drive a car by reading a book.

The final section of the book provides guidelines for creating original programs. Basic routines for the important computer functions are described so that the reader may insert the specific details of the particular job that is being programed to create a wide variety of different programs.

As a final note, Radio Shack's TRS-80 comes in two models. The "beginner's" model is called Level I. This is the specific programing language described in this book. The second model is called Level II. This is a more sophisticated and versatile computer. The Payroll Program has been written for the limitations of the Level I model, but the necessary substitutions to make it function on Level II are thoroughly explained. Again, to apply the Payroll Program to other computer models, consult the owner's manual for the specific operating and programing procedures of the brand being used.

Using This Book

This book has been designed as an introduction to the wonders of micro-computer programing as well as a reference guide for the development of original programs.

The reader may find it more convienent to take this book apart and put it in a three ring binder. In this way other information on programing may be stored with it. To "unbind" the book, open it at around the middle, say page 40. Pull open the spine and cut through it with a sharp knife. The pages may then be pulled off one at a time like taking the pages off a tablet of scratch paper. After the pages have been removed, they may be punched and put into a binder.

THE COMPUTER

Micro-computers consist of three basic parts: a keyboard, a video display screen, and a magnetic storage device such as a cassette tape recorder. Information is entered on the keyboard. It is then transmitted to the computer's brain. This brain is the electronic circuitry which is usually inside the keyboard. The brain transmits the information to a video display screen so that the computer operator may see what is happening. The information in the computer's brain may then be sent to the storage device (the tape recorder) to be recorded for use at a later time.

Basic Operating Procedures

The first step in understanding how to program a computer is to learn the basic operating procedures. The best way to learn the operating procedures is to sit down at a computer and run it.

1. Turning the Computer On

To start, the computer's components must be connected together following the instructions in the owner's manual. Then the computer may be turned on. When the computer has been properly hooked up and turned on, it will display the word READY and a Prompt Cursor (>_). This is the signal that the computer is ready to go to work.

Step 1. Turn On. The Display Shows:

READY

>_

---

2. Typing and Correcting

Information is put into the computer by typing on the keyboard. Type in the word HELLO. The video screen of the computer will display whatever is typed in. If HELLO is misspelled, the spelling may be erased by pressing the Back Space Key (◄—). The Back Space Key will move one space to the left everytime it is pressed. This erases, letter by letter, anything that has been typed in. The spelling may then be corrected. This is the basic procedure for talking to the computer.

Step 2. Type In:

HELLO

Step 3. Back Space to the "E". The Display Shows:

HE

Step 4. Type In:

HEELO

Step 5. Back Space to the "E". The Display Shows:

HE

Step 6. Type In:

HELLO

3. Entering Information

The computer will not respond to the information that has been typed in until the Enter Key is pressed. With HELLO typed in, press the Enter Key. The computer prints WHAT? drops down two lines and prints READY. The Prompt Cursor appears on the following line.

Computers respond to specific instructions, not to idle chit chat. The computer has not been told how to respond to HELLO so it prints what is called an error message. The error message occurs when information is entered that the computer does not understand.

Step 7. Press the Enter Key. The Display Shows:

HELLO
WHAT?

READY
>_

4. Computer Instructions

Computers are very obedient about following instructions. More so than any human being will ever be. But they must be told very precisely in their own specific language exactly what they are expected to do. For example, tell the computer to print the word HELLO.

Step 8. Type In:

PRINT "HELLO"

Once again, the computer will not respond to what has been typed in until the Enter Key is pressed. This allows corrections to be made to any line that has been typed in up until the Enter Key is pressed.

Step 9. Press the Enter Key. The Display Shows:

```
READY
PRINT "HELLO"
HELLO

READY
>_
```

The computer was told to print the word HELLO so it did. The quotation marks around the word HELLO were not printed. These quotation marks are a computer signal. They indicate to the computer the exact sequence of letters and/or numbers that are to be printed. The READY and the Prompt Cursor which appear below the HELLO indicate that the computer is ready for its next instruction.

5. Clearing the Display

The Video Screen can become quite crowded with information. To erase the screen, the Clear Key is pressed. The Clear Key may be used at the discretion of the operator.

Step 10. Type In:

```
PRINT "HELLO"
```

Step 11. Press the Clear Key. Press the Enter Key. The Display Shows:

```
HELLO

READY
>_
```

6. Accuracy

Accuracy is very important if the computer is to run properly. The spelling of words must be exact. The punctuation has to be the correct computer signals. An entire program will function incorrectly, or not at all, if a comma (,) is used instead of a semi-colon (;). Human beings can interpret what is meant by a statement if it is incorrectly phrased or poorly punctuated. Computers will not. Try the following intentional errors to see how the computer responds. Type in each line, one at a time, and press the Enter Key right after that line has been typed in.

Step 12. Type In and Enter:	The Computer Will Print:
PRRINT "HELLO"	WHAT?
PRINT HELLO	−.5
	WHAT?
PRINT 'HELLO'	WHAT?
PRINT, "HELLO"	WHAT?
PRINT "HEELO"	HEELO

Line 1. The instruction is incorrectly spelled. The computer does not know what to do, so it says WHAT? This is the error message. Different computers will have different error messages, but the idea holds true for all computers. They do not operate from incorrect instructions.

Line 2. The quotation marks are left off. The quotation marks are a signal to the computer to print exactly what has been typed in. If these are left off, the computer will treat the information as a number. The computer is not exactly sure what kind of a number HELLO is, so it prints the error message WHAT?

Line 3. Single quotation marks are used here instead of double quotation marks. This is an incorrect computer signal, so the computer prints the error message.

Line 4. A comma is included after the PRINT Instruction. This is an incorrect placement for the punctuation mark. The computer is merciless in its requirement for total accuracy, so it prints the error message.

Line 5. In this case, the incorrect spelling was placed inside the quotation marks, so the computer spelled the word exactly the same as the dummy who put it there in the first place.

7. Numeric Values

Information not enclosed between quotation marks is treated by the computer as numeric values. In this function, the computer will act like a pocket calculator or an adding machine.

Step 13.   Press the Clear Key.   Type In and Enter:
4+5

The computer displays nothing after this simple addition problem because it was not told what to do.

Step 14. Type In and Enter:	The Computer Will Print:
PRINT 4+5	9

Now the computer has printed the answer to the addition problem, but it did not print the problem itself. It is good computer programing procedure to have the computer explain what it is doing as it is doing it.

Line 1 in Step 15 below first puts the addition problem between quotation marks. The computer will print this information exactly as it is typed in. A semi-colon (;) is then typed in. This semi-colon is a computer signal that tells the computer there are two parts to the instruction. Then the actual problem the computer is to solve is typed in without quotation marks. The information between quotation marks is printed character by character but the information not between quotation marks is seen by the computer's brain as a single numeric value.

Line 2 of Step 15 is a subtraction problem using the same numbers. This illustrates an important concept about spacing information on the display screen.

Step 15. Type In and Enter:	The Computer Will Print:
PRINT "4+5="; 4+5	4+5= 9
PRINT "4−5="; 4−5	4−5=−1

The computer has left a space between the equal sign and the 9 but no space between the equal sign and the -1. The computer prints numeric values in the first space after the information in quotation marks. The first space, however, is reserved for the sign of the number. The minus sign is printed but the positive sign is assumed. To place a space between the equal sign and the minus sign, the Space Bar must be pressed after the equal sign and before the quotation mark as shown in Step 16 on the next page.

Step 16. Type In and Enter:	The Computer Will Print:
PRINT "4—5= "; 4—5	4—5= —1

8. Math Functions

Radio Shack's TRS-80 in Level I performs the following math functions when it is given the appropriate computer signal as shown below. It performs these calculations in a very precise sequence. First the computer reads an instruction from left to right and does all of the multiplication and division. It then returns to the left and performs all of the addition and subtraction calculations.

Function	Symbol
Addition	+
Subtraction	—
Multiplication	*
Division	/

Step 17. Type In and Enter:	The Computer Will Print:
PRINT 3*5+6+4*2	29

The computer has followed this sequence:

1) 3 * 5 = 15 (a)

2) 4 * 2 = 8 (b)

3) 15 (a) + 6 + 8 (b) = 29

To specify a different sequence than this, the calculations to be performed first should be placed between parentheses.

Step 18. Type In and Enter:	The Computer Will Print:
PRINT 3*5+(6+4)*2	35
PRINT 3*5+(6+4*2)	29
PRINT 3*(5+(6+4)*2)	75

The computer has followed this sequence:

1.
1) 6 + 4 = 10 (a)
2) 3 * 5 = 15 (b)
3) 10 (a) * 2 = 20 (c)
4) 15 (b) + 20 (c) = 35

2.
1) 4 * 2 = 8 (a)
2) 6 + 8 (a) = 14 (b)
3) 3 * 5 = 15 (c)
4) 15 (c) + 14 (b) = 29

3.
1) 6 + 4 = 10 (a)
2) 10 (a) * 2 = 20 (b)
3) 5 + 20 (b) = 25 (c)
4) 3 * 25 (c) = 75

To keep track of complicated combinations of calculations, write the problem out on a piece of paper and draw boxes around the calculations to be performed first. The boxes indicate the location of the parentheses.

3 * 5 + 6 + 4 * 2

Parentheses must be kept in pairs or an error message will occur.

Step 19. Type In and Enter:	The Computer Will Print:
PRINT (3*5+(6+4)*2	WHAT?

9. Variables

A Variable is a storage location in the computer's memory that allows information to be established in one instruction and acted upon later. There are two types of Variables, Numeric Variables and String Variables. Numeric Variables store the total numeric value of the information that they are given. String Variables remember the specific "string" of letters, numbers, and symbols that they are given.

The storage location for each Variable is assigned a specific name. The names of the Variables may be a single letter, a combination of two letters, or a combination of a letter and a single numeral. The Variable A is different from the Variable B, etc. In addition, String Variables are assigned a dollar sign as a part of their name to distinguish them from Numeric Variables. Thus, the Variable A is a Numeric Variable. The Variable A$ is a String Variable.

Information may be stored in a Variable by typing the name of the Variable, an equal sign, and the information that is to be stored. The information to be stored in a String Variable must be enclosed between quotation marks or an error message will occur.

The information in a given Variable is "variable" because the computer only remembers the last information that was put into the Variable. All previous information is dropped out of the computer's memory.

In Step 20 below, each line gives the computer two sets of instructions. The first instruction establishes the value of the Variable. The second instruction tells the computer to print the information stored in the Variable. The two instructions are separated by a computer signal, the colon (:). The computer will read and act upon what is to the left of the colon first before proceeding to the instruction to the right of the colon.

Step 20. Type In and Enter:	The Computer Will Print:
A=5: PRINT A	5
A$="HELLO":PRINT A$	HELLO
A=5:PRINT "A=";A	A= 5

The third line in Step 20 improves upon the first line because it describes what the computer is printing. The computer prints A= before it prints the value stored in the Variable A.

The semi-colon in the third line tells the computer that there are two parts to the PRINT Instruction. (See page 15.)

Special Note: Some computers use the phrase LET to establish the value in a Variable. For example, LET A = 5. With Radio Shack's TRS-80, this phrase is optional.

The mathematical calculations that were previously written with parentheses in Step 18 may now be written using Variables to establish the proper sequence for the calculations.

$$3 * 5 + (6 + 4) * 2$$

$$3 * 5 + (6 + 4 * 2)$$

$$3 * (5 + (6 + 4) * 2)$$

Step 21. Type In and Enter:	The Computer Will Print:
A=6+4:PRINT 3*5+A*2	35
A=6+4*2:PRINT 3*5+A	29
A=6+4:B=5+A*2:PRINT 3*B	75

This illustrates a very important fact about working with a computer. Any given task may usually be approached in several different ways. It is up to the person working on the computer to determine the specific instructions as he or she sees fit. A program may be judged right or wrong by whether or not it produces the correct answers to the problem.

There are, however, some programs which are more efficient than others for both the computer and the operator. For example, in the last calculation, using parentheses only required 19 keys to be pressed to enter the information. The same calculation using Variables required 21 keys. This is an insignificant difference on this short program, but as the instructions become more involved, there can be quite a difference.

Basic Programing Procedures

Up to this point, the computer has done what it was told to do on a one shot basis. One of the main advantages of computers is that they may be given a series of instructions which they will repeat as frequently as they are asked. The process of writing a given set of instructions for the computer is called programing.

Programs may be very simple or incredibly complicated. The more involved the instructions, the more effective the computer will be in saving human time.

1. Program Lines

The computer is programed by putting instructions into Lines. A Line is created by preceding a computer instruction with a Line Number. The Line Number signals the computer to hold the instruction in its memory and to act upon the instruction when it is told to do so. In other words, computer instructions without Line Numbers call for immediate execution as soon as the Enter Key is pressed but they will not be stored in the computer's memory. Computer instructions with a Line Number will not be executed when the Enter Key is pressed, but they will be stored in the computer's memory.

The computer will start reading the instructions from the smallest Line Number and progress to the largest Line Number unless it is given an instruction to follow a different sequence.

A program line is created by typing in a Line Number, the instruction, typing in the desired information, and pressing the Enter Key. The Enter Key stores the line in the computer's memory and returns the Prompt Cursor to the left side of the screen so that another line may be entered.

IMPORTANT NOTE - The computer needs to know the difference between the number zero and the letter O. This is indicated by putting a slash through the zero, Ø.

```
NEW
10 PRINT "HELLO"
20 PRINT "4+5=";4+5
30 PRINT "2*(4+5)=";2*(4+5)
```

Notice that the word NEW is typed in without a Line Number. This instruction tells the computer to clear everything out of its memory that may have strayed in during the earlier operations. Do not type NEW into the computer as a program is being developed or all of the instructions will be lost.

2. Running the Program

The program is now stored in the computer's memory. The computer will not run the instructions until it is told to do so. To start the program, type in the word RUN without a Line Number and press the Enter Key.

Step 2.   Type In and Enter:

```
RUN
```

Step 3.   The Computer Will Print:

```
HELLO
4+5=  9
2*(4+5)=  18

READY
>_
```

3. Corrections

Everyone makes mistakes. There are two ways to correct any error that is typed in.

1. Before the Enter Key is pressed, the line may be changed by Back Spacing to the error and retyping the line.

2. After the Enter Key is pressed, the line is stored in the computer's memory. To change this memory, the Line Number must be typed again. The correct line is then typed and entered.

Step 4.   Type In and Enter:

40 PRINT"SO WHATT"

50 PRRINT"DON'T SAY THAT"

Step 5.   Press the Clear Key.   Type In and Enter:

RUN

Step 6.   The Computer Will Print:

HELLO

4+5=9

2*(4+5)=18

SO WHATT

WHAT?

   50 P?RRINT "DON'T SAY THAT"

In Line 40, the error is inside quotation marks, so the computer faithfully misspells WHAT just as it was told to do.

In Line 50, however, the computer's instruction was misspelled so the computer did not know what to do. Retype these two lines correctly.

Step 7.   Type In and Enter:

40 PRINT"SO WHAT"

50 PRINT"DON'T SAY THAT"

RUN

4. Deleting Lines

To remove an instruction from the computer's memory, type in only the Line Number and press the Enter Key. This makes the computer forget the instruction all together.

Step 8.   Type In and Enter:

40

50

RUN

---

5. Adding Lines

Notice that the Line Numbers used in creating the program so far have been spaced at intervals of 10. This is good programing procedure because as the program develops, it may be necessary to add instructions to an earlier part of the program.

Step 9.   Press the Clear Key.   Type In and Enter:

15 PRINT "HOW ARE YOU?"

RUN

Step 10.   The Computer Will Print:

HELLO

HOW ARE YOU?

4+5=9

2*(4+5)=18

---

6. Clearing the Display

The Clear Key has been pressed quite a bit to keep the Display Screen clear. This function of erasing the screen may be added as an instruction in the program by typing in CLS. Retype Line 10 so that every time the program is run, the computer's first instruction is to clear the screen.

Step 11.   Type In and Enter:

10 CLS:PRINT "HELLO"

RUN

---

7. Listing the Program

The program may be run as many times as desired by typing in RUN and pressing the Enter Key. Each time, the computer will follow the instructions it has been given in exactly the same way. The instructions will not appear on the screen during this time. To examine the program that is in the computer's memory, type in the instruction LIST without a Line Number and press the Enter Key.

Step 12.   Type In and Enter:

LIST

Step 13.   The Computer Will Print:

10 CLS:PRINT "HELLO"

15 PRINT"HOW ARE YOU?"

20 PRINT"4+5=";4+5

30 PRINT "2*(4+5)=";2*(4+5)

---

8. Input Information

The program as it is now written is fine as long as all the information that is needed is contained inside the program. Most programs, however, will require some kind of information that must be added during the run of the program. This is achieved by giving the computer an INPUT Instruction.

An INPUT Instruction is created by typing in a Line Number, the instruction INPUT and then a Variable. The Variable may be either a Numeric Variable, such as A, or a String Variable, such as A$.

Step 14.   Type In and Enter:

20 INPUT A$

RUN

Step 15.   The Computer Will Print:

HELLO

HOW ARE YOU?

?

The computer processes the instruction to print HELLO and drops to the next line where it is told to say HOW ARE YOU? On the next line, it encounters the INPUT Instruction which stops the program and waits for information to be entered on the keyboard. After it receives this information, it will proceed with the program.

Step 16.   Type In and Enter:

FINE

Nothing is done with the information put into the Variable because the computer has no instructions to do anything with A$. Also, when the computer gets to the INPUT Instruction, all that appears on the screen is a question mark. After a coffee break, the person running the computer could forget what this question mark is waiting for. Retype the program as shown in Step 17. Be careful to follow the exact sequence of characters using all of the semi-colons and quotation marks just as they appear. In Line 5Ø there are six parts to the PRINT Instruction. The first part is to print 2*(, the second part is to print the numeric value of the Variable A, the third part is to print a plus sign, the fourth part is to print the numeric value of the Variable B, the fifth part is to print)= and the final part is to print the numeric value of the problem.

Step 17.   Type In and Enter:

```
20 INPUT "A=";A
30 INPUT "B=";B
40 PRINT A; "+"; B; "="; A+B
50 PRINT "2*("; A; "+"; B; ")="; 2*(A+B)
RUN
```

Each time the computer comes to an INPUT Instruction, it waits for a number to be entered from the keyboard. First, a value is assigned to the Variable A and then a value is assigned to the Variable B.

Step 18. When the Computer Prints:	Type In and Enter:
A=?	21
B=?	3456

Step 19. The Computer Will Print:
21+3456=3477
2 * (21+3456)=6954

If a letter is entered instead of a number, the computer makes up its own value and processes the information accordingly. In some computers, Radio Shack's Level II for example, if a letter is entered into an INPUT Instruction that has a Numeric Variable, an error message will occur.

Step 20. When the Computer Prints:	Type In and Enter:
READY	RUN
A=?	21
B=?	X

Step 21. The Computer Will Print:
21+.5=21.5
2 * (21+.5)=43

When a number in the thousands is entered, no comma is used. The comma is a special computer signal that will cause the computer to read the information to the left of the comma and ignore the information to the right of the comma.

Step 22. When the Computer Prints:	Type In and Enter:
READY	RUN
A=?	21
B=?	3,456

Step 23. The Computer Will Print:
21+3=24
2 * (21+3)=48

The computer may be run as many times as desired putting in new values for A and B on each run. When the new value is entered, the old value is dropped out of the computer's memory.

9. GOTO Instructions

One of the most versatile aspects of computers is that they may be given instructions which alter the sequence of lines that the computer normally follows. One of these instructions is GOTO which tells the computer to go to a specific Line Number in the program.

A GOTO Instruction is created by typing in a Line Number, the instruction GOTO, and then the Line Number in the program that the computer is to proceed to.

Step 24.   Type In and Enter:

60 GOTO 20
RUN

With this instruction the program is changed into a continuous loop. After the first pass through the program, the computer will reach Line 6Ø which redirects the program to Line 2Ø. Notice that HELLO and HOW ARE YOU? are only printed once. This is because they are printed by Lines 1Ø and 15 and the computer avoids these lines by going directly to Line 2Ø. The Clear Key must be pressed to clear the display screen because the CLS is also bypassed.

10. Breaking Into a Program

To stop this program from running in an endless loop, press the Break Key. READY and a Prompt Cursor will appear indicating that the computer is ready for a new instruction.

Step 25.   Press the Break Key.

---

11. END Instructions

END Instructions are used to "end" the run of a program. This instruction will be a necessary part of many programs. The END Instruction in Step 26 below is in Line 1ØØ. Line 9Ø is a PRINT Instruction which tells the computer operator what is happening.

Step 26.   Type In and Enter:

90 PRINT"THE END"
100 END

---

12. IF THEN Instructions

　　IF THEN Instructions are another way of changing the direction a program will follow. GOTO Instructions always send the program to a given Line Number. IF THEN Instructions may or may not change the sequence of a program depending on the information that is being processed. The IF THEN Instruction is very important because it allows programs to operate with flexibility rather than always following the same steps.

　　In the example below, when the Variable A is given the numeric value -1, the program is redirected to Line 9∅ which will print THE END and then drop to Line 1∅∅ which will end the program. In this example, the numeric value -1 is reserved as a stopping device to break the program out of its endless loop. In other words, the −1 is used instead of the Break Key.

Step 27.　Type In and Enter:
25 IF A = −1 THEN 9∅ RUN

Step 28.　When the Computer Prints:	Type In and Enter:
A=? B=?	21 3456
A=?	−1

Step 29.　The Computer Will Print:
THE END READY >_

13. FOR NEXT Loops

The computer may also be asked to repeat a specified series of instructions for a given number of times and then to proceed with the rest of the program. This is done with a FOR NEXT Instruction. The FOR NEXT Loop is created by putting the FOR Instruction at the beginning of the sequence of instructions that are to be repeated and by putting the NEXT Instruction at the end of this sequence.

The FOR Instruction is created by typing in a Line Number, the word FOR, and then an equation which establishes the number of times the steps are to be repeated, I = 1 TO 3. The Variable I is the counting device. The instruction to the right of the equal sign tells the computer to count from 1 to 3 using I to hold the current value.

The NEXT Instruction is put at the end of the sequence of instructions that are to be followed. It will return the program to the FOR Instruction until the specified number of passes has been made. After the last specified pass, 3 in this example, the program proceeds with the rest of the program.

Step 30.   Type In and Enter:

```
15 FOR I = 1 TO 3
60 NEXT I
RUN
```

Program Storage

The computer's memory has certain limitations:

1. It does not remember instructions unless they are given a Line Number.

2. It remembers only the last information that is entered into a given Variable. All previous information is dropped out of the computer's memory.

3. It does not remember the information in a Variable after the run of a program has ended.

4. It will forget all the instructions in a program and all the information in the Variables when the power to the keyboard is turned off.

These lapses in the computer's memory are actually a strength because they increase the computer's versatility. The short memory of the Variables allows an infinite amount of information to be processed through a given program. The loss of the entire program allows an infinite number of programs to be entered into the computer so that it may do a variety of tasks.

The problem, of course, is that frequently the programs or the information in the Variables will need to be saved for use at a later time. This can be done by storing the data on a magnetic storage device such as a cassette tape.

The procedure for storing the information in Variables must be written into the program. This will be described in a later section. The procedure for saving a program is described here. This procedure saves only the names of the Variables. It does not store the information contained inside the Variables.

IMPORTANT NOTE - Cassette tapes are sensitive to any kind of magnetic field. Placing a cassette tape near a magnetic field will distort or remove any information that may be stored on it. The power transformer of Radio Shack's TRS-80 generates a magnetic field. Do Not place cassette tapes near the transformer.

1. Saving Programs

The instruction CSAVE is used to store programs on cassette tapes. Before entering this instruction into the computer, prepare the tape recorder as described below.

Step 1. Take the cassette tape to be used to store the program and look through the open slot in the edge of the casing. See if the leader portion of the tape is exposed. The leader is a different color from the body of the tape. It is not magnetically sensitive and will hold no information. By hand, wind the cassette until the leader is no longer visible in the opening.

Step 2. Put the cassette into the tape recorder and adjust the volume controls as specified in the Owner's Manual of the computer.

Step 3. Put the tape recorder in record by pressing both the Play Button and the Record Button simultaneously.

Step 4. Type in CSAVE on the computer keyboard and press the Enter Key. The instruction in Level II is CSAVE "S".

The computer will automatically start the tape recorder, record the program, and turn the tape recorder off. The video screen will display READY and the Prompt Cursor when the process is completed.

Step 5. Press the Stop Button on the tape recorder to release the Play and Record Buttons.

Every program should be saved on two separate tapes. One tape will be used to put the program into the computer. The second tape is used as a backup to the first tape in case the first tape is accidentally erased or misplaced. Keep this second tape in a safe location.

2. Checking the Computer's Memory

The computer has retained the program in its memory throughout this procedure. Type in LIST and enter this instruction. The computer will display the last program that was entered.

Now type in the instruction NEW and press the Enter Key. If LIST is typed in now, the screen will remain blank because the NEW Instruction cleared the computer's memory.

The number of brain cells a computer has for remembering information is limited. However, unlike people, it is possible to purchase additional memory to expand the computer's abilities. To determine how much memory the computer has available, type in the instruction PRINT MEM. The computer will display on the Video Screen the amount of memory that is available for running a a given program. The units of a computer's memory are called bytes and they are approximately equivalent to one typed character. Make a note of the amount of memory that is available at this time.

3. Loading Programs

The program that is stored on the cassette tape may be put back into the computer's memory by using the CLOAD instruction.

Step 1. Rewind the tape recorder to the beginning of the tape.

Step 2. Put the tape recorder in play by pressing the Play Button. Adjust the volume control as specified in the Owner's Manual for the computer.

Step 3. Type in CLOAD on the computer keyboard and press the Enter Key.

The computer will automatically turn on the tape recorder. As soon as the tape recorder reaches the beginning of the program, the computer will start flashing a signal in the upper left hand corner of the video screen. After the program has been loaded, the computer will turn off the tape recorder and display a READY and the Prompt Cursor.

Step 4. Press the Stop Button of the tape recorder to release the Play Button.

The memory available in the computer has now been decreased by the program that has just been loaded. To see the program, type in LIST and press the Enter Key. To see how much memory is left, type in PRINT MEM. Subtract the amount of memory currently available from the memory previously available when the computer had no program. The difference between these two quantities is the amount of memory used to store the current program.

THE COMPUTER PROGRAM

The first part of this book has shown the basics of how a computer functions. The rest of the book will concentrate on the process of creating programs to make the computer perform specific jobs.

There are many different ways to create programs but the computer follows a definite sequence of logical steps to achieve any given task. This book will break programs down into these logical steps and then show how to create specific portions of a program to accomplish these individual functions. After all of the separate parts are completed, the computer will automatically follow the entire program.

The format this book follows divides programs into four different parts. 1. Fixed information is stored in one part of the program. 2. Information that varies is added into the program in a different part of the program. 3. The program manipulates the information to perform the assigned task. 4. The results of the manipulation are presented for use in different ways.

The best way to understand how this program format works is to see it applied to solving a specific task. The example described here is a Payroll Program. Understanding how this program works will enable the reader to develop many different original programs by applying the same principles.

It is very important to keep the different parts of the program format separate. This is accomplished by assigning blocks of Line Numbers to specific functions. The Line Numbers in the Payroll Program have been predetermined to let the individual parts of the program work by themselves without having the entire program typed in. Once all of the parts have been entered into the computer, the program will work as a cohesive whole. It is very important to follow the Line Numbers exactly as they are shown in the Payroll Program. The last section of the book will describe how to assign Line Numbers to original programs.

The Payroll Program will use a lot of the computer's available memory. A computer with 4K of memory will only be able to enter the program up to the Advanced Calculation section. The entire program will require 9K units of memory. To minimize the amount of memory used in entering the program, press the Space Bar only where absolutely necessary for clarity. Each time the Space Bar is pressed, another unit of memory is used.

NOTE: This program has been specifically designed to operate on Radio Shack's TRS-80 Level I. The necessary substitutions to make it operate on Level II are described and listed in the boxes labeled Level II Substitution as shown below.

Level II Substitution

To apply this program and programing format to other computer models, first become thoroughly familiar with the specific operating procedures and programing language of that computer. Then, work at understanding the logic of the descriptions in this book. Finally, translate the specific language here into the langauge that particular model understands.

The Program Description

The first step in creating any program is to think through the job that the computer is to perform. This will include the general purpose of the program, the information the computer will need to operate the program, the calculations and program manipulations the computer will need to make, and the type of output that the computer will need to create to complete the task.

1. General Purpose

First, determine the overall purpose of the program in very general terms. The overall purpose of the Payroll Program is to take the hours worked by the employees during a given pay period and generate the necessary information to write pay checks.

2. Stored Information

Fixed information that will not vary from one run of the program to the next should be written into the program so that it does not have to be typed in each time.

In the Payroll Program, the information that does not change is the data about the employees. This information includes the employee's name, rate of pay, and tax data: marital status and number of tax exemptions.

Other information may be included as necessary to make the program run as efficiently as possible. One example of this is the Employee Code in the Payroll Program. This code establishes whether or not the worker is currently employed by the company. This code is used to drop past employees from the calculations for the current payroll but to retain them for the end-of-the-year tax statements.

Other information, such as deductions for union dues or special savings plans, may be added to the Payroll Program as applicable.

3. Input Information

Information that changes from one run of the program to the next will be introduced into the program through INPUT instructions. In the case of the Payroll Program, this information will be the number of hours the employees worked during a given pay period. This sample program is specifically written for a biweekly pay period. The hours for each week are entered separately so that the computer will be able to automatically calculate all overtime that exceeds 40 hours a week.

4. Program Calculations

After the information is entered into the program, it will be manipulated to produce the desired results. In the Payroll Program, the information is manipulated to calculate the gross pay of each employee. The payroll deductions will be determined and subtracted from this amount, and the resulting net pay will be calculated.

The specific Payroll Program described here is based on the following circumstances:

> U.S. Income Tax (1979)
> Social Security (1979)
> California State Income Tax (1979)
> California State Disability Insurance

5. Program Output

After the program has manipulated the information, the results may be used in a variety of ways. In the Payroll Program, the information will be displayed on the Video Screen so that pay checks may be written. The information will also be stored for later use in preparing W-2 forms, end-of-the-quarter and end-of-the-year tax statements.

This program could be used on a TRS-80 Level II with a Line Printer to automatically print the payroll checks.

This is a sample program only. Not every payroll is figured on an hourly basis or a biweekly schedule. Taxes vary from year to year and state to state. The principles described here may be used to adapt, alter, and adjust the program to the specific requirements of the user. The resulting program must be run in parallel with existing accounting/bookkeeping systems for a sufficient length of time to verify that the program is producing accurate results.

Stored Information

To clearly visualize the information that is to be stored in a given program, write it out in tabular form such as the table shown below for the Payroll Program.

Emp #	Name	Pay	Mar. Status	Tax Exemp.	Code
1	Harrison	3.25	1	1	1
2	Samuels	3.50	3	4	1
3	Johnson	3.75	2	2	1

The table above gives all of the necessary information about each employee for the payroll calculations. The first column is for the Employee Number. This number will be used by the computer to keep the employee files separate and accurate. The second column is for the Employee's Name and the third column is for the rate of pay. The fourth column establishes the employee's Marital Status using the following numeric coding: 1 - single, 2 - married, 3 - head of the household. This information is assigned numbers because the computer can process numbers much more quickly and efficiently than words. The fifth column is the number of Tax Exemptions the employee claims. The last column is the Employee Code with 1 being the code for a currently employed worker and -1 being the code for a former employee.

1. Storing Information

Information may be stored in a program by using a DATA Instruction. The DATA Instruction is created by typing a Line Number, then the word DATA, followed by the specific sequence of information that was established in the table described above. Each piece of information must be separated by a comma. Each DATA line must follow exactly the same sequence of information.

Step 1. Type In and Enter:

```
NEW
510 DATA 1, HARRISON, 3.25, 1, 1, 1
520 DATA 2, SAMUELS, 3.50, 3, 4, 1
530 DATA 3, JOHNSON, 3.75, 2, 2, 1
```

2. Retrieving Stored Information

The information in a DATA Instruction is retrieved for use in the program by a READ Instruction. The READ Instruction is created by typing a Line Number, the word READ, and then a series of Variables separated by commas. The Variables of the READ Instruction must coincide with the information in the DATA Instruction. The names used for the Variables (A, B, etc.) may be anything that makes sense to the programer.

Step 2.   Type In and Enter:

7040 READ E, A$, H, M, X, C

For the Payroll Program, the READ Instruction assigns the Employee Number to the Variable E, the Employee Name to the String Variable A$, the Hourly Pay to the Variable H, the Marital Status to the Variable M, Tax Exemptions to the Variable X, and the Employee Code to the Variable C. Notice that the Employee Name is the only information that requires a String Variable. All other information is assigned to Numeric Variables.

3. Displaying Stored Information

The READ Instruction will not by itself print the information in the DATA Instruction. To do this, a PRINT Instruction must be used.

The information will be easier to read and comprehend if it is displayed by the computer as a table. This type of display format may be created by using a TAB Instruction. The TAB Instruction acts like the tab button on a typewriter. It establishes the position on the Video Screen where the computer will start to print the information.

Notice in Step 3 below that the first instruction in Line 7ØØØ is to clear the display screen (CLS). The computer is then told to start printing in space 22 by the TAB Instruction. Radio Shack's TRS-80 has 64 spaces across the screen. Try changing this Tab Number and see how it changes the display. *Apple 40 spaces.*

Step 3.   Type In and Enter:

7000 CLS:PRINT TAB(22); "EMPLOYEE RECORDS"
RUN

Step 4.   The Computer Will Print:

                    EMPLOYEE RECORDS

Now the computer may be asked to print the body of the table. Line 7Ø1Ø has two PRINT Instructions separated by a colon. The first PRINT Instruction has nothing to print so it prints a blank display line. The second PRINT Instruction starts on the following display line. Notice the blank line in Step 6.

The headings of the columns in tables are spaced by using TAB Instructions between each heading of the PRINT Instruction. Normally, PRINT Instructions written on different program lines, as in 7Ø1Ø and 7Ø11, would be printed on separate lines of the display screen. The semi-colon at the end of Line 7Ø1Ø is a signal to the computer to print the next program line on the same display line as Line 7Ø1Ø.

Line 7Ø5Ø prints the information that is retrieved by the READ Instruction in Line 7Ø4Ø. This information is placed in the proper columns of the table by the TAB Instructions.

Step 5.   Type In and Enter:

```
7010 PRINT:PRINT"#"; TAB(5); "NAME"; TAB(20); "PAY";
7011 PRINT TAB(28); "MAR STATUS"; TAB(41); "TAX EX"; TAB(50); "CODE"
7050 PRINT E; TAB(5); A$; TAB(19); H; TAB(31); M; TAB(42); X; TAB(50); C
RUN
```

Step 6.   The Computer Will Print:

EMPLOYEE RECORDS

#	NAME	PAY	MAR STATUS	TAX EX	CODE
1	HARRISON	3.25	1	1	1

The information on only one employee has been printed because there is only one READ Instruction. This may be corrected by adding a FOR NEXT Loop that will repeat both the READ Instruction in Line 7Ø4Ø and the PRINT Instruction in Line 7Ø5Ø.

Step 7.   Type In and Enter:

```
7030 FOR I=1 TO 3
7060 NEXT I
RUN
```

Step 8.   The Computer Will Print:

EMPLOYEE RECORDS

#	NAME	PAY	MAR STATUS	TAX EX	CODE
1	HARRISON	3.25	1	1	1
2	SAMUELS	3.50	3	4	1
3	JOHNSON	3.75	2	2	1

Line 7Ø3Ø establishes a loop based on three employees. The FOR NEXT Loop will be used in several parts of the program to read the information in the employee data files. If, at a later date, more employees are added, each of the FOR NEXT Loops would have to be rewritten for the new number of employees. Therefore, it is more efficient to write the FOR NEXT Loop using a Variable as in the revised Line 7Ø3Ø of Step 9 below. The value of this Variable should be set as one of the first Line Numbers in the program, Line 2Ø in Step 9. In this way, when new employees are added, all that needs to be changed is Line 2Ø.

Another factor that must be compensated for is the fact that a DATA Instruction may normally only be read once during the run of a program. The RESTORE Instruction in Line 7Ø2Ø of Step 9 resets the DATA and the READ Instructions so that they may begin at the beginning. This may be compared to taking a file out of a filing cabinet. A given file may only be removed once unless it is replaced. The RESTORE Instruction is this refiling.

The last line in Step 9 is a LIST Instruction which will enable the reader to examine the entire segment of the program that displays the employee records. The instruction LIST is followed by the Line Number 7ØØØ. This tells the computer to start Listing the program from Line 7ØØØ. To examine the earlier part of the program which included the DATA Instructions, leave off the 7ØØØ.

Step 9.   Type In and Enter:

```
7030 FOR I = 1 TO W
20 CLS: W = 3
7020 RESTORE
LIST 7000
```

```
7000 CLS:PRINT TAB(22); "EMPLOYEE RECORDS"
7010 PRINT:PRINT"#"; TAB(5); "NAME"; TAB(20); "PAY";
7011 PRINT TAB(28); "MAR STATUS"; TAB(41); "TAX EX"; TAB(50); "CODE"
7020 RESTORE
7030 FOR I=1 TO W
7040 READ E, A$, H, M, X, C
7050 PRINT E; TAB(5); A$; TAB(19); H; TAB(31); M; TAB(42); X; TAB(50); C
7060 NEXT I
```

LEVEL II – Level II uses slightly different LIST Instructions which require a dash to be entered after the 7000. Otherwise, all that will be Listed is the Line 7000.

Level II Substitution

LIST 7000-

4. Changing Stored Information

Information that is stored in the computer program may be altered by retyping the program line containing the information which is to be changed.

Changes to the DATA Lines in the Payroll Program will occur when an employee is given a raise, changes marital status, adds or loses dependents, quits or gets fired. New employees may also be hired which would require new DATA Instructions be added to the program.

If a change is made to the program, the program should be rerecorded on a cassette tape so that subsequent runs of the program will retain the revisions.

5. Labeling Stored Information

Information that is stored in a DATA Instruction should be carefully labeled in the program. In this way, when information is added at a later date, it will follow the same sequence and structure as the earlier information. A REM Instruction may be used for this labeling.

REM is short for Remark. This instruction prints information when a program is listed. It does not affect the run of the program. Line 5ØØ below indicates the beginning of the Employee Record File. Lines 5Ø1 through 5Ø6 describe the information that is stored in the Employee Records and shows the Variables that are used to retrieve the data. Lines 5Ø7 and 5Ø8 describe the sequence that the information in the DATA Instructions follow. Line 5Ø9 describes the Variable W and shows how Line 2Ø should be adjusted when additional employees are added.

Step 11.   Type In and Enter:

500 REM - EMPLOYEE RECORDS

501 REM - 1. EMPLOYEE NUMBER (E)

502 REM - 2. EMPLOYEE NAME (A$)

503 REM - 3. HOURLY PAY (H)

504 REM - 4. MARITAL STATUS (M): 1=SINGLE, 2=MARRIED, 3=HEAD OF HOUSE

505 REM - 5. NUMBER OF TAX EXEMPTIONS (X)

506 REM - 6. EMPLOYEE CODE (C): 1=CURRENT, −1 = PAST EMPLOYEE

507 REM - ENTER NEW EMPLOYEE AS BELOW

508 REM - 000 DATA E, A$, H, M, X, C

509 REM - W = NO. OF EMP THIS YEAR. ENTER IN LINE 20: 20 W=3

NOTE: Since Line 5Ø4 is longer than 64 characters, do not press the Enter Key until after the word HOUSE. The computer will automatically drop down to the next display line after 64 characters have been typed in.

Input Information

Information that will vary from one run of the program to the next should be added to the program through INPUT instructions. In the case of the Payroll Program, the information that will be added is the number of hours each employee worked during a given pay period.

The Variable that is used to hold the employee hours is called an Array. In Radio Shack's Level I computer there is only one Array which is named A( ). An Array can generate a vast "array" of Variables because each different Numeric Value that is placed between the parentheses of the Array generates a different Variable. In other words, A(1) is a different Variable than A(2), etc. The Array is very versatile because the specific Numeric Value in the Array can be changed during the run of the program to provide different storage locations in the computer's memory.

For the Payroll Program, the Variable E, which is the Employee Number, will be used inside the parenthesis of the Array. This means that each Employee Number creates a new Variable. This keeps the hours of each employee distinctly separate from the hours of the other employees.

1. Inputing Information

As mentioned earlier, the Payroll Program described here is for a biweekly pay period. The hours for each employee are entered as a total for each week. This allows the program to automatically calculate overtime for each week.

The Array Variables used for the first week will be $A(2\emptyset+E)$ where E is the Variable for the Employee Number. The second week will be stored in $A(4\emptyset+E)$. There is a gap of 20 between each week so that 20 employees may be kept in this program. In other words, A(21) is the Variable for the first week's hours of the first employee. A(22) is the Variable for the first week's hours of the second employee, etc.

The INPUT Instructions for the Payroll Program are listed in Step 1 below. Notice that the INPUT Instructions are labeled WEEK 1 and WEEK 2 so that the information being requested will be clear to the computer operator.

Step 1.   Type In and Enter:

140 INPUT"WEEK 1 "; A(20+E)

150 INPUT"WEEK 2 "; A(40+E)

The INPUT Instructions are dependent on the information in the stored data files because the Employee Number, E, is used to establish the Array. Therefore, a READ Instruction must precede the INPUT Instructions. All of the Data in the file must be read even though only the Employee Number is being used at this point. This is the only way the computer can keep the information straight in its brain.

Step 2.   Type In and Enter:

110 READ E, A\$, H, M, X, C

There is more than one employee so a FOR NEXT Loop must be established to read all of the employee files.

Step 3.   Type In and Enter:

100 FOR I=1 TO W

230 NEXT I

The program also needs to tell the person running the program which employee is currently being processed, Step 4. Notice in this step there is a space between the BY and the final quotation mark. If this space is not there, the BY and the employee's name will be run together when this line is printed.

Step 4.   Type In and Enter:

130 PRINT"TOTAL HOURS WORKED BY "; A\$

One final refinement is to have the program skip over past employees. This feature was established by assigning a 1 to current employees and a -1 to former employees (see page 37). This information is retrieved by the Variable C in the READ Instruction. Line 12Ø says that if a person is a former employee, skip over the INPUT Instructions (Lines 14Ø and 15Ø) and go directly to the next employee, Line 23Ø. If C is not -1, the program will automatically drop down to the next program line.

Step 5.   Type In and Enter:

120 IF C = −1 THEN 230

LIST

Step 6.   The Computer Will Print:

20 CLS: W=3

100 FOR I=1 TO W

110 READ E, A$, H, M, X, C

120 IF C= −1 THEN 230

130 PRINT"TOTAL HOURS WORKED BY "; A$

140 INPUT"WEEK 1 "; A(20+E)

150 INPUT"WEEK 2 "; A(40+E)

230 NEXT I

LEVEL II - Whereas Level I has only one Array, A( ), Level II has many. The Level I Array may generate as many Variables as the computer's brain can remember. But the Level II Arrays are assigned an initial allotment of ten Variables each, A(Ø) to A(9). A(2Ø+E) will generate an error message. To override this feature, a DIM Instruction may be used to establish the number of Variables that may be used in a given Array. DIM is short for the Dimension of the Array. To establish the Dimension of an Array, type in the instruction DIM, the Array name, and inside the parentheses state the number of Variables that are to be used with that particular Array. The following substitution must be made for Line 2Ø to allow this program to function on a Level II computer.

Level II Substitution

20 CLS: W=3: DIM A(200)

Another possible variation for this Payroll Program in Level II is to assign different Arrays for different information. For example, the Array W1(E) could be used to hold the hours for Week 1 instead of A(2Ø+E). The Array W2(E) could be used for the hours of Week 2. This would allow more than 20 employees to be put into this program providing the computer has enough memory. This substitution is not essential, however, to the functioning of the program. It will be left up to the reader to make these substitutions as desired.

Step 7. Type In and Enter:

RUN

Step 8. The Computer Will Print:

TOTAL HOURS WORKED BY HARRISON
WEEK 1?

Sample hours may now be typed in for each employee to test this part of the program.

2. Displaying Input Information

It is a good idea to display the information that has been put into a program to make sure that it has all been entered correctly.

The format used to display the Input Information is basically the same format that was used to display the Employee Records. The main difference is that Line 2Ø4Ø jumps over any employee who is no longer employed. Line 2Ø5Ø is a temporary line in the program which sets the value of A(E) at zero. Later, this Array will hold the gross pay for the employees.

LEVEL II - Level II users may want to substitute the Array GP(E) for A(E). Once again, this substitution is not essential for the operation of this program on Level II computers.

```
2000 CLS: RESTORE:PRINT TAB(15); "THIS PAY PERIOD'S PAYROLL":
PRINT
2010 PRINT"#"; TAB(5); "NAME"; TAB(20); "HOURS"; TAB(30); "AT";
2011 PRINT TAB(40); "GROSS PAY"
2020 FOR I=1 TO W
2030 READ E, A$, H, M, X, C
2040 IF C=-1 THEN 2070
2050 A(E)=0
2060 PRINT E; TAB(5); A$; TAB(19); A(20+E)+A(40+E); TAB(29); H; TAB(39)
; A(E)
2070 NEXT I
```

One very essential addition to any display format is to stop the program so that the computer operator may view the information. As the program is now written, the computer will proceed through the 2000 series of instructions and automatically proceed to the next Line Number which is Line 7000. The first instruction in Line 7000 is CLS which clears the display screen. The 2000 series of instructions will appear as a brief flash of light on the screen.

INPUT Instructions stop a program until information is typed in on the keyboard and entered. Line 2090 will stop the program until a key, such as Y is pressed and entered. This allows the computer operator to control the length of time the program pauses for the display.

```
2090 PRINT:PRINT:INPUT"CONTINUE (Y)"; A
RUN
```

LEVEL II – Level II has a nice modification that simply allows the Enter Key to be pressed after an INPUT Instruction for a program to continue. It is not necessary to press any other key.

Level II Substitution

```
2090 PRINT:PRINT:INPUT"CONTINUE"; A
```

To see how the display routine operates, type in 4Ø hours for each week of each employee. After all of the information has been entered, the screen will display the information as seen in Step 11.

Step 11.   The Computer Will Print:

THIS PAY PERIOD'S PAYROLL

#	NAME	HOURS	AT	GROSS PAY
1	HARRISON	8Ø	3.25	Ø
2	SAMUELS	8Ø	3.50	Ø
3	JOHNSON	8Ø	3.75	Ø

CONTINUE (Y)

Corrections

It is very easy to make a mistake when information is being typed into the program. Once the Enter Key is pressed, the information, including the errors, will be stored in the computer's memory. The following routine will allow corrections to be made to the Input Information.

The principle behind correcting an error is to place the exact Variable containing the error back into an INPUT Instruction. The correct value is entered and the wrong value is dumped out of the computer's memory.

There are two INPUT Instructions for the initial entry of the information, so there must be two INPUT Instructions for the corrections.

Step 1. Type In and Enter:

```
3150 INPUT"HOURS FOR WEEK 1"; A(20+E)
3170 INPUT"HOURS FOR WEEK 2"; A(40+E)
```

The next step is to write an INPUT Instruction that will tell the computer which INPUT to correct. Line 3120 asks whether Week 1 or Week 2 is to be corrected. This information is put into the Variable A.

Step 2. Type In and Enter:

```
3120 A=0:INPUT "CORRECTIONS TO WEEK 1 OR 2"; A
```

Based on the information that is entered into the Variable in Line 3120, the program must be directed to either Line 3150 or Line 3170 which contain the two correction INPUT Instructions.

In order to do this, a new computer instruction will be used, ON GOTO. The ON GOTO Instruction is written by typing in a Line Number, the word ON, a Variable, the instruction GOTO and then a series of Line Numbers separated by commas. The ON part of this instruction reads the value in the Variable. The GOTO part uses this value to count over to the appropriate Line Number.

In this ON GOTO Instruction, if the number in the Variable A is 1, the computer will count over to the first Line Number in the GOTO portion of the instruction. The program will be directed to this line, Line 3150. If the value in the Variable A is 2, the computer will count over to the second Line Number indicated in the GOTO Instruction, Line 3170. On any other value for the Variable A, the program will drop down to the next program line, Line 3140. Line 3140 sends the program back to Line 3120. Either a 1 or a 2 must be entered into Line 3120 or the computer will just continue to send the program in circles from Lines 3120 to 3140.

If the program is sent to Line 3150, the correction will be made to Week 1. The program then automatically drops down to the next Line Number, Line 3170. This means that if a correction is made to Week 1, the program will automatically ask for a correction to Week 2. To correct this problem, the program must jump over Line 3170 when it leaves Line 3150.

Now one week may be corrected without correcting the other week. But what if both weeks must be corrected? This leads to a very important computer routine that will be used in many programs. This is a simple Yes/No decision that must be made by the computer operator. After one week is corrected, the program will proceed to Line 3180 where the operator will be asked if the other week must be corrected.

Line 3180 sets a Yes answer, Y, as a Numeric Value of 1 and a No answer, N, as 2. This is followed by an INPUT Instruction that asks for the appropriate decision. Line 3190 uses an ON GOTO Instruction to direct the program to the correct Line Number based on the operator's decision. Line 3120, the Yes answer, directs the program to the beginning of the correction routine. Line 3210, a No answer will be the continuation of the program. If an inappropriate response is entered, Line 3200 returns the program to the beginning of the Yes/No routine.

LEVEL II - Level II makes a much stronger distinction between letters and numbers entered from the keyboard. The Yes/No routine described above will not function in Level II. The substitution below will allow Level II programs to function properly.

Level II Substitution

```
3180 INPUT"CORRECT ANOTHER WEEK (Y/N)"; Y$:IF Y$="Y"THEN 3120
3190 IF Y$="N" THEN 3210
```

The INPUT Instruction requires a String Variable because a letter entered into a Numeric Variable, such as A, will create an error message. An IF THEN Instruction determines if the answer is Y, in which case the program is directed to Line 3120 (the beginning of the correction routine). Otherwise, the program drops to the next line, Line 3190. This line checks to see if the answer is "N". If it is, the program is directed to Line 3210 which will continue the program. Do not use the shift key when typing in the Y or the N because that is a different character to the computer than the unshifted Y or N.

The Correction Routine in the Payroll Program is written as a Subroutine. Subroutines are established with a GOSUB Instruction. The GOSUB Instruction is similar to the GOTO Instruction in that the program is directed to a specific line in the program. The difference between the two is that the GOSUB Instruction will make the program boomerang back to where it came from once the Subroutine is completed.

```
200 GOSUB 3120:REM - CORRECTIONS
3220 RETURN
3000 END
```

Line 2ØØ establishes the GOSUB Instruction (Go to Subroutine) which sends the program to the Correction Subroutine.   Line 322Ø is a RETURN Instruction.   This instruction tells the computer that the Subroutine is completed and it is time to go back to the rest of the program.   If there is more than one GOSUB Instruction, the RETURN Instruction will return the program to the specific GOSUB Line that initiated the Subroutine.

Line 3ØØØ is an END Instruction which stops the run of the program.   This END Instruction stops the program from going to the Correction Routine after the Display Routine in Lines 2ØØØ to 2Ø9Ø.

Another Yes/No routine may now be inserted into the first part of the program so that the program operator may decide either to make corrections or to proceed with the program if corrections are not required.

```
170 A=0:Y=1:N=2:INPUT"CORRECTIONS (Y/N)"; A
180 ON A GOTO 200, 230
190 GOTO 170
LIST
```

LEVEL II - The same Yes/No substitution that was described on the previous page must be made.

The LIST Instruction must also be modified because in Level II this instruction will display the entire program.   The LIST Instruction indicated below will stop the program at Line 23Ø.

Level II Substitution

```
170 INPUT"CORRECTIONS (Y/N)"; Y$:IF Y$="Y"THEN200
180 IF Y$="N" THEN230
LIST −230
```

Step 9. The Computer Will Print:

```
20 CLS: W=3
100 FOR I=1 TO W
110 READ E, A$, H, M, X, C
120 IF C= -1 THEN 230
130 PRINT"TOTAL HOURS WORKED BY "; A$
140 INPUT"WEEK 1 "; A(20+E)
150 INPUT"WEEK 2 "; A(40+E)
170 A=0:Y=1:N=2:INPUT"CORRECTIONS (Y/N)"; A
180 ON A GOTO 200, 230
190 GOTO 170
200 GOSUB 3120:REM - CORRECTIONS
230 NEXT I
```

Line 17Ø establishes the decision. If the decision is to make a correction, the program is directed to Line 2ØØ. This line sends the program to the Correction Subroutine. If the decision is not to make a correction, the program is directed to Line 23Ø which continues the program. Notice that a REM Instruction is included in Line 2ØØ to label the specific Subroutine the program is being directed to.

Simple Calculations

The program may now be told to do a simple calculation using the information that has been entered. This simple calculation will allow the computer to run through the functions of the program in the proper sequence. The more advanced calculations required to determine overtime and withholding information will be described as the final step in creating the Payroll Program.

1. Calculating Gross Pay

The Gross Pay of the employees is determined by adding the hours for both weeks together and multiplying this figure by the hourly rate of pay.

Step 1. Type In and Enter:

```
1000 A(E)=H * (A(20+E)+A(40+E))
```

In Line 1000, the Gross Pay is stored in the Array A(E). Notice that the two weekly totals for the hours, A(20+E) and A(40+E), are added together inside parentheses before they are multiplied by the hourly rate of pay stored in the Variable H.

2. Calculations as a Subroutine

The calculations are written as a Subroutine so that they may be reached directly after the information is initially entered or later in the program if a correction is made to the hours.

Step 2. Type In and Enter:

```
220 GOSUB 1000:REM - CALCULATIONS
3210 GOSUB 1000:REM - CALCULATIONS
1010 RETURN
```

Both Lines 22∅ and 321∅ will send the program to the calculations. Line 22∅ is in the initial part of the program. Line 321∅ is in the Correction Subroutine. Line 1∅1∅ will return the program to either Line 22∅ or Line 321∅ depending on which line originates the GOSUB Instruction.

3. Adjusting the Initial Program Lines

Several lines will need to be adjusted so the computer will follow the proper sequence of functions in the program.

Step 3.   Type In and Enter:

180 ON A GOTO 200, 220
210 GOTO 230
300 GOTO 2000

Level II Substitution

180 IF Y$="N" THEN 220

Line 18∅ must be rewritten. Originally, this line sent the program either to the Correction Subroutine via Line 2∅∅ or to the next employee, Line 23∅. This line must be changed to send the program to the calculations, Line 22∅, before the next employee is processed. In other words, the program first picks up the hours for a given employee; then it may or may not go to the corrections; the calculations are performed; and finally the program is directed to the next employee.

Line 21∅ jumps over the Calculation Subroutine, Line 22∅, if the program is returning from the Correction Subroutine, Line 2∅∅. The Correction Subroutine sends the program to the Calculation Subroutine in Line 321∅. There is no need to have the same calculations performed a second time.

Line 3∅∅ sends the computer to the Payroll Display routine, Lines 2∅∅∅ to 2∅9∅, after all of the employees hours have been entered in the initial part of the program.

4. Totaling Gross Pay

The Gross Pay for all of the employees may be added together to determine the total payroll.

The principle of totaling the information in a given Array is a very important concept to understand because it will be used in many programs.

Remember, a Variable is used to hold information. The information in a Variable is normally dropped out of the computer's memory when new information is introduced. However, the computer will first calculate any mathematical expressions before it stores a Numeric Value in a given Variable. Line 2050 shows how the initial value of a Variable may be included in the calculations that determine the new value of the Variable. Each pass of the FOR NEXT Loop picks up a new value in A(E) and adds this to the earlier total.

Step 4.   Type In and Enter:

```
2012 T=0
2050 T=T+A(E)
2080 PRINT:PRINT"THE TOTAL PAYROLL IS $";T
RUN
```

When this totaling procedure is used, it is necessary to start the initial value of the Variable at zero because other values may have strayed into the Variable and they would be added into the calculations. This is achieved in Line 2012.

The results of the totaling are printed by Line 2080.

The location of these steps in a given routine is important. The Variable must be set at zero before the FOR NEXT Loop starts. The line that adds the values in the Array must be inside the FOR NEXT Loop and it must come after the READ Instruction which establishes the current Variable of the Array. The instruction to print the total must be placed after the end of the FOR NEXT Loop.

Multiple Functions

The Payroll Program follows the basic sequence of steps that many programs use. 1. Information is put into the program. 2. Corrections, if necessary, may be made to the information. 3. Calculations are performed. 4. The results are displayed.

Actually, the results of a given program may be used in many different ways. The information may be displayed on the Video Screen in different formats depending on the required uses. The information may be stored on magnetic recording devices for use at a later time. And, with printing equipment, various forms, checks, and statements may be printed.

Not all of these functions are required for each run of the program and the sequence in which these functions are needed may vary from one run to the next. The operator must therefore be able to select which function of the program the computer should follow at a given time. This is done by a Multiple Function Selection routine.

The specific functions for the Payroll Program are as follows.

1. Display the Contents - This is the function that displays the information which has been put into the program (Lines 2ØØØ to 2Ø9Ø).

2. Make Additional Corrections - After all of the information is entered, it may be necessary to change some of the data.

3. Total the Payroll - This routine displays the results of the calculations the computer makes. The format is displayed so that pay checks may be written. A routine is included which totals all of the various withholding classifications.

4. Store the Payroll - The payroll information is stored on cassette tape so that it may be used later to generate tax statements and W-2 forms.

5. Retrieve the Payroll - Anytime the information in a program is stored, there should be another part of the program which will retrieve it.

6. Display the Employee Records - This is the routine which displays the contents in the DATA Instructions (Lines 7ØØØ to 7Ø6Ø).

1. Selecting Program Functions

First, a series of lines must be written that will print the different functions of the program. The first line in this series, Line 3ØØ, includes a provision to clear the display screen, CLS.

Step 1.   Type In and Enter:

300 CLS:PRINT"DISPLAY CONTENTS (1)"

310 PRINT"ADDITIONAL CORRECTIONS (2)"

320 PRINT"TOTAL PAYROLL (3)"

330 PRINT"STORE PAYROLL (4)"

340 PRINT"RETRIEVE PAYROLL (5)"

350 PRINT"DISPLAY EMPLOYEE RECORDS (6)"

Now an INPUT Instruction is required so that the operator may select the appropriate function. This information will be stored in the Variable A of Line 37Ø.

Step 2.   Type In and Enter:

370 A=0: INPUT A

Next, the program must be sent to the appropriate function. Each function is written as a Subroutine. An ON GOSUB Instruction will select the appropriate Line Number for the beginning of the desired routine.

The ON GOSUB Instruction works just like the ON GOTO Instruction described earlier. The ON part of the instruction picks up the Numeric Value in the Variable A and counts over to the appropriate Line Number in the GOSUB portion of the instruction. A RETURN Instruction at the end of each Subroutine sends the program back to the GOSUB Instruction.

Step 3.   Type In and Enter:

380 ON A GOSUB 2000, 3000, 4000, 5000, 6000, 7000

When the program returns from a given Subroutine it drops down to the next program line. This is Line 4ØØ which redirects the program to the beginning of the Multiple Function Selection process.

2. Ending the Program

After the program is run through all of the functions desired, it will need an END Instruction.

Line 36∅ establishes the END Instruction as the last line of the Multiple Function Selection list. When 7 is entered into the INPUT Instruction in Line 370, the ON GOSUB Line counts over to the seventh Line Number in the GOSUB portion of the instruction. There are only 6 Line Numbers, so the program drops down to the next line, Line 39∅. This line sees the 7 and sends the program to the END Instruction.

A deliberate entry of 7 into the Multiple Function Selection routine is the only thing that will end this program. This prevents the program from accidentally ending at the wrong time.

3. Converting Functions to Subroutines

In order for the program to be tried out as it was being developed, two functions, Displaying Contents and Displaying Employee Records, were not written as Subroutines. These two functions may now be changed to Subroutines by adding RETURN Instructions to the end of each function.

The Employee Record Display was originally written without a pause control. This routine ends with the highest Line Number so the program stops here because there is nowhere else to go. However, when a RETURN Instruction is included, an INPUT Instruction must be added to stop the program so that the operator may view the information on the Video Screen.

Step 7. Type In and Enter:

7070 PRINT:PRINT:INPUT"CONTINUE (Y)"; A
RUN

LEVEL II - The Y may be dropped because it is not necessary to press anything other than the Enter Key for a Level II INPUT Instruction.

Level II Substitution

7070 PRINT:PRINT:INPUT"CONTINUE "; A

Run the program to try out the Multiple Function Selection routine. The only valid selections at this time are 1, 6, and 7 because the rest of the program has not been completed.

4. Expanding the Correction Subroutine

The Correction Subroutine was originally written to correct information immediately after it was entered. It must now be expanded so that corrections may be made after all of the information is entered. To make a correction later in the program, the computer operator must be able to select which employee's data is going to be changed.

First, the Correction Routine will print a table that displays all of the employee's names and their hours for both weeks.

```
3000 CLS:RESTORE:PRINT"#"; TAB(5); "NAME";
3001 PRINT TAB(20); "HOURS FOR WEEK 1, WEEK 2"
3010 FOR I=1 TO W
3020 READ E, A$, H, M, X, C
3030 IF C= −1 THEN 3050
3040 PRINT E; TAB(5); A$;
3041 PRINT TAB(29); A(20+E); TAB(36); A(40+E)
3050 NEXT I
```

Line 3000 clears the screen (CLS) and refiles the employee data (RESTORE). Then Lines 3000 and 3001 print the column headings for the information.

Lines 3010 and 3050 set up a FOR NEXT Loop which reads the employee data, Line 3020, and prints this information under the appropriate heading, Line 3040. Line 3041 prints the information stored in the Variables for the hours, A(20+E) and A(40+E).

```
3060 END
RUN 3000
```

#	NAME	HOURS FOR WEEK 1, WEEK 2	
1	HARRISON	0	0

Step 9 displays the format created by these instructions. The RUN Instruction bypasses the first part of the program and starts with Line 3000. All of the employees will not be displayed because the value of the Variable W, which sets up the number of passes the FOR NEXT Loop makes, is in Line 20 which was bypassed. The END Instruction in Line 3060 is a temporary instruction to stop the computer from continuing the program.

LEVEL II - An error message will be generated when this is run in Level II because the DIM Instruction, which establishes the Dimension of the Array in Line 3041, is in Line 20 which was bypassed. The general format of the table may still be seen.

When this routine is run as a part of the complete program, the computer operator may see which employee's hours are to be changed. Line 3Ø6Ø then asks the operator to select the appropriate employee by typing in the Employee Number. This information is stored in the Variable G.

Step 11.   Type In and Enter:

```
3060 RESTORE:PRINT:INPUT"CORRECTIONS TO EMPLOYEE #"; G
```

Now the computer will be told to search through the DATA Instructions and pull out the data of the employee whose hours are to be changed. This type of computer routine is very useful because it has applications in many programs.

A FOR NEXT Loop is set up to run through the employee data files. Each Employee Number which is stored in the Variable E is compared to the Employee Number of the worker whose hours are to be changed, the Variable G. If the two Employee Numbers match, the program is directed to the main portion of the Correction Subroutine.

The remainder of the FOR NEXT Loop is bypassed. Therefore, the correct information is retained in the Variables of the READ Instruction.

Step 12.   Type In and Enter:

```
3070 FOR I=1 TO W
3080 READ E, A$, H, M, X, C
3090 IF E=G THEN 3120
3100 NEXT I
3110 GOTO 3060
RUN
```

Line 311Ø is a safety check. A valid Employee Number must be entered in Line 3Ø6Ø or the program will just keep looping from Line 3Ø6Ø to 311Ø.

This computer routine can be compared to the process of retrieving a file from a filing cabinet. The person looking for the file starts at the beginning of the file drawer and searches through the files, the FOR NEXT Loop, until the correct file is found. The file is then removed from the drawer, Line 3Ø9Ø.

The program may now be run so that the complete Correction Subroutine can be tested. To quickly pass through the first part of the program, press the two key every time the program stops for an INPUT Instruction.

5. Initial Program Information

It is a good idea to label the beginning of any program. Line 1Ø below is a reminder to turn off the tape recorder after the program has been loaded into the computer. Line 3Ø prints the name of the program. Lines 4Ø and 5Ø establish the specific dates of the pay period being processed. This information will be used to label the payroll data when it is recorded on cassette tape.

Step 13.   Type In and Enter:

```
1Ø INPUT"TURN OFF THE TAPE RECORDER (Y)"; A

3Ø CLS:PRINT TAB(12); "PAYROLL PROGRAM":PRINT

4Ø INPUT"BEGINNING DATE OF PAY PERIOD"; B

5Ø INPUT"ENDING DATE OF PAY PERIOD"; D:PRINT
```

LEVEL II - The Y may be dropped because it is not necessary to press anything other than the Enter Key for a Level II INPUT Instruction.

Level II Substitution

```
1Ø INPUT"TURN OFF THE TAPE RECORDER "; A
```

6. Program Sophistication

One of the best aspects of the new personal computers is the fact that the person who is running a given program may adapt that program to meet the specific situation of the job being handled.

In the Payroll Program, for example, if most of the employees work a specified number of hours for most pay periods, the information may be written into the program so that the computer operator is not typing in the same information all the time.

Lines 6Ø to 9Ø allow the operator to select the mode that is to be followed for a given pay period.

Step 14.   Type In and Enter:

```
6Ø PRINT "THIS PAY PERIOD FOLLOWS:"

7Ø INPUT "1. STANDARD HOURS, 2. VARIED HOURS"; A

8Ø ON A GOTO 700, 100

9Ø GOTO 60
```

```
700 CLS:PRINT "DO NOT DISTURB, I'M WORKING"
710 REM - EMPLOYEES' STANDARD HOURS
720 A(21)=40:A(41)=40:REM - HARRISON
730 A(22)=40:A(42)=40:REM - SAMUELS
740 A(23)=40:A(43)=40:REM - JOHNSON
```

Line 700 prints DO NOT DISTURB because the complete payroll calculations for all of the employees will take seconds to process. During this time the computer will not respond to information typed in on the keyboard. This message alerts the operator to what is happening.

Lines 720 to 740 supply the information that, up to now, has been entered through the INPUT Instructions. The number between the parentheses is determined by adding the value of the week to the Employee Number. For example, A(20+E) is the Array for the first week, 1 is the Employee Number for Harrison. Therefore, A(21) is the Variable for the hours of the first week for Harrison.

```
900 FOR I=1 TO W
910 READ E, A$, H, M, X, C
920 GOSUB 1000
930 NEXT I
940 GOTO 300
RUN
```

To calculate the pay and deductions, the information must be processed through a FOR NEXT Loop, Lines 900 to 930. This loop first reads the employee data files and then goes to the Calculation Subroutine.

Line 940 sends the program directly to the Multiple Function Selection routine. The first part of the program is thereby completely bypassed.

Changes to the hours worked in a week which vary from the standard hours may be accomplished by using the Correction Subroutine.

Other computer functions may be developed as the needs arise. The new personal computers are incredibly versatile in their ability to adapt to new circumstances.

Information Storage

Frequently, the information created by a program will be needed at a later date. This section describes how to store and retrieve the information contained in the Variables and Arrays on a cassette tape. Only the values in the Variables and the Arrays are stored. The names of the Variables and Arrays are not recorded. This is similar to the way DATA Instructions operate.

1. Storing Information

Information is stored on cassette tape by using a PRINT # Instruction. The data in the instruction must be separated by a specific sequence of semi-colons, quotation marks, and commas, see Line 5Ø2Ø.

Step 1.   Type In and Enter:
5020 PRINT # B; ", "; D; ", "; W
5050 PRINT # E
5060 PRINT # A(E)

Line 5Ø2Ø records the beginning and ending dates of the pay period from the Variables B and D. The number of workers is recorded from the Variable W. This information is important because the FOR NEXT Loop which retrieves the employee information must be adjusted as new employees are added.

The Employee Number is recorded from the Variable E. This number will be used to label information in the Arrays when the data is retrieved to insure that the data is assigned to the correct employee.

Line 5Ø6Ø records the information contained in the Arrays.

LEVEL II - The instruction for storing information on tapes in Level II is PRINT #-1. The data only needs to be separated by commas.

Level II Substitution

```
5020 PRINT # −1, B, D, W
5050 PRINT # −1, E
5060 PRINT # −1, A(E)
```

There is more than one employee so a FOR NEXT Loop is added around the employee information.

Step 2.   Type In and Enter:

```
5030 FOR E=1 TO W
5070 NEXT E
```

Former employees are not processed through current payroll calculations. As a safety measure, it is a good idea to make sure their Variables have not picked up stray values. Line 5040 sets the Gross Pay for former employees at zero.

Step 3.   Type In and Enter:

```
5040 IF C= −1 THEN A(E)=0
```

When the information is ready to be stored on cassette tape, the tape recorder will have to be prepared. This includes putting a tape into the tape recorder, adjusting the volume control, and putting the tape recorder in record by pressing the Play and the Record Buttons. Lines 5000 and 5010 alert the computer operator to make sure the tape recorder is ready. 5010 is an INPUT Instruction so that the program will not proceed until the operator is ready.

Step 4.   Type In and Enter:

```
5000 CLS:PRINT"PREPARE TO STORE PAYROLL"
5010 INPUT"IS THE TAPE RECORDER IN RECORD (Y)"; A
```

LEVEL II - As described earlier, the Y may be dropped because it is not necessary to press anything other than the Enter Key for a Level II INPUT Instruction. This substitution will be performed several times in this section with no further explanation.

Level II Substitution

5010 INPUT"IS THE TAPE RECORDER IN RECORD "; A

The computer will automatically turn on the tape recorder, store the information, and turn off the tape recorder. The following lines will alert the computer operator that the information has been stored and that the Stop Button should be pressed to release the Record and Play Buttons.

Step 5.   Type In and Enter:

5080 PRINT"THE PAYROLL IS STORED"
5090 INPUT"IS THE TAPE RECORDER TURNED OFF (Y)"; A

Level II Substitution

5090 INPUT"IS THE TAPE RECORDER TURNED OFF "; A

The function of storing information on tape is written as a Subroutine. A RETURN Instruction must be included to return the program to the Multiple Function Selection routine.

Step 6.   Type In and Enter:

5100 RETURN
RUN

Run the program using the standard hour function so that each employee has 80 hours for the pay period. Record this information on a cassette tape.

The best way to store data created by several runs of a given program is to have one cassette tape designated specifically to store the information from that program. Start recording the first run of the program at the beginning of the tape. Leave the tape as it is after the information is recorded and store the tape in a safe place (away from magnetic fields). To store the next run of the program, place the tape back into the recorder and start recording the information from the second run of the program right after the information from the first run. Be careful not to rewind the tape before the second run is recorded or the information from the first run will be erased. If anything, advance the tape slightly after the first run so that there is a gap of unrecorded tape between the first program run and the second.

2. Retrieving Information

The instruction for retrieving information that has been recorded on a cassette tape is INPUT #. These instructions must be written in exactly the same way the information was recorded. For example, Line 5Ø2Ø (Step 1) stored three pieces of data. The corresponding line in the retrieval routine, Line 6Ø2Ø, must contain three Variables to recover the information. The next two PRINT # Instructions (Lines 5Ø5Ø and 5Ø6Ø) recorded one piece of data each. The Variables and Arrays in INPUT # Instructions are separated by commas.

Step 7. Type In and Enter:

6020 INPUT# B, D, W

6080 INPUT# E

6090 INPUT# A(E)

LEVEL II - The instruction for retrieving data in Level II is written INPUT #-1. The information is separated by commas.

Level II Substitution

6020 INPUT# −1, B, D, W

6080 INPUT# −1, E

6090 INPUT# −1, A(E)

To retrieve the employee data, a FOR NEXT Loop is used to repeat the INPUT # Instructions in Lines 6Ø8Ø and 6Ø9Ø. The value of the Variable W is established by the INPUT # Instruction in Line 6Ø2Ø. In this way, the FOR NEXT Loop is adjusted to make the correct number of passes for the particular pay period being recovered.

Step 8.   Type In and Enter:

```
6070 FOR I=1 TO W
6100 NEXT I
```

An important feature in a retrieval function is to be able to select the particular batch of data desired. The Payroll Program data is labeled according to the beginning and ending dates of the specific pay period. This information was retrieved by the Variables B and D in Line 6Ø2Ø (see Step 7). It is printed on the Video Screen by Line 6Ø3Ø.

Step 9.   Type In and Enter:

```
6030 PRINT"THIS PAY PERIOD STARTS"; B; "AND ENDS"; D
```

Now the computer operator may determine if this is the pay period that is to be retrieved.

Step 10.   Type In and Enter:

```
6040 A=0:INPUT"RETRIEVE: 1. THIS PAY PERIOD, 2. ANOTHER"; A
6050 ON A GOTO 6070, 6010
6060 GOTO 6040
```

If the current pay period is to be retrieved, a 1 is entered into the Variable A. The program proceeds to Line 6Ø5Ø. The ON Instruction counts over to the first Line Number in the GOTO Instruction which is Line 6Ø7Ø. This is the beginning of the FOR NEXT Loop which picks up the employee data.

If another pay period is desired, the operator enters a 2 into the Variable A of Line 6Ø4Ø. The program drops to Line 6Ø5Ø and the ON Instruction counts over to the second Line Number in the GOTO Instruction. This is Line 6Ø1Ø, the beginning of the retrieval routine. The computer operator may now adjust the cassette tape forward or backward to a different pay period.

There are no clear indications on a cassette tape where one batch of information starts and the other ends. For this reason the Totaling Program (which is described later) starts from the beginning of the tape, the first pay period of the year, and proceeds to the end of the recorded information. To recover a pay period in the middle of the recorded information, it is necessary to loop between Lines 6Ø1Ø and 6Ø5Ø until the correct pay period is discovered.

When the Payroll Retrieval function is selected, the computer operator must put the correct tape into the tape recorder, adjust the volume control, and put the tape recorder in play by pressing the Play Button. Lines 6ØØØ and 6Ø1Ø alert the operator to do this.

IMPORTANT - Do not put the tape recorder in record when information is going to be retrieved because this will erase the information on the tape.

Step 11.   Type In and Enter:

6000 CLS:PRINT"PREPARE TO RETRIEVE THE PAYROLL"

6010 INPUT"IS THE TAPE RECORDER IN PLAY (Y)"; A

After the information has been retrieved, the operator needs to press the Stop Button on the tape recorder to release the Play Button. The program is returned to the Multiple Function Selection routine by Line 613Ø.

Step 12.   Type In and Enter:

6110 PRINT"THIS PAY PERIOD IS RETRIEVED"

6120 INPUT"IS THE TAPE RECORDER TURNED OFF (Y)"; A

6130 RETURN

RUN

Level II Substitution

6010 INPUT"IS THE TAPE RECORDER IN PLAY "; A

6120 INPUT"IS THE TAPE RECORDER TURNED OFF "; A

Run the program and enter zero hours for each employee. Then retrieve the information that was previously stored on the cassette tape (page 67). When the retrieved information is displayed by the Display Contents function, the hours will be zero but the Gross Pay will be for 80 hours. This is because the hours were not stored on the tape, only the pay was stored.

Advanced Calculations

The program has only performed the simplest calculations with the employee hours so far. This was done so that the basic program format could be explained and tried out without typing in all of the repetitive data required for tax calculations.

Depending on personal needs and interests, the reader may use the information in this section in several ways. If the reader is not specifically interested in a payroll program, then the section may just be read for an understanding of the computer routines that are used. For a better understanding of the computer functions, try out the calculations which do not require a lot of data to be entered such as the calculations for overtime, the Social Security deductions and the U.S. Income Tax deductions. To see the full power of the computer, or to create a functioning Payroll Program, type in all of the data described.

The calculations described in this section are: 1. Overtime, 2. Federal Income Tax withholding, 3. Social Security Tax withholding, 4. California State Income Tax withholding, 5. California State Disability Insurance, and 6. Net Pay. The results of each of the calculations will be held in a specific Array. The names of each of the deductions will be abbreviated in the display of the program. These Arrays and their abbreviations are listed below. The box to the right indicates Array names for Level II that could be used for programs that are to have more than 20 employees. This is not a necessary substitution to make the program run properly so it is left to the reader to make the appropriate changes.

Name	Abbreviation	Array	Level II
Federal Income Tax	FIT	$A(8\emptyset+E)$	FT(E)
Social Security Tax	FICA	$A(6\emptyset+E)$	SS(E)
State Income Tax	SIT	$A(1\emptyset\emptyset+E)$	ST(E)
State Disability Insurance	SDI	$A(12\emptyset+E)$	SD(E)
Net Pay		$A(14\emptyset+E)$	NP(E)

The first step in developing the calculations is to set the various Arrays at zero and then create a display format that will print the results of the calculations. In this way, when a particular calculation has been entered into the program, the program may be run and the results of the calculation viewed.

```
1050 A(120+E)=0
1100 A(60+E)=0
1200 A(80+E)=0
1300 A(100+E)=0
1600 A(140+E)=0
1010
1900 RETURN
```

This step sets the values of the Arrays at zero and changes the RETURN Instruction from Line 1010 to Line 1900.

1.   Displaying the Payroll

The display routine shown below follows the standard format used in the earlier display routines (see pages 39 to 40).

```
4000 CLS: RESTORE:PRINT TAB(26); "PAYROLL":PRINT
4010 PRINT"#"; TAB(5); "NAME"; TAB(18); "GROSS"; TAB(28); "FIT";
4011 PRINT TAB(36); "FICA"; TAB(43); "SIT"; TAB(49); "SDI"; TAB(56);
"NET"
4020 T=0:U=0:V=0:P=0:L=0
4030 FOR I=1 TO W
4040 READ E, A$, H, M, X, C
4050 IF C=−1 THEN 4090
4060 PRINT E; TAB(5); A$; TAB(17); A(E); TAB(27); A(80+E); TAB(35);
4061 PRINT A(60+E); TAB(42); A(100+E); TAB(48); A(120+E); TAB(55);
A(140+E)
4080 T=T+A(E):U=U+A(80+E):V=V+A(60+E):P=P+A(100+E):L=L+A(120+E)
4090 NEXT I
4100 PRINT:PRINT TAB(20); "– – – – – – – – – – – – – – – – – – – – – – – – – –"
4110 PRINT TAB(17); T; TAB(27); U; TAB(35); V; TAB(42); P; TAB(48); L
4120 PRINT:PRINT:INPUT"CONTINUE (Y)"; A
4130 RETURN
RUN
```

Line 4000 clears the screen and prints the title of the display.

Lines 4010 and 4011 set up the headings for the columns of the table.

Line 4020 sets the value of the five Variables at zero. These Variables will be used to total each of the withholding columns (see Line 4080).

Lines 4030 and 4090 establish the FOR NEXT Loop.

Line 4040 is the READ Instruction for the employee data.

Line 4050 makes the program jump over the display for any past employee.

Lines 4060 and 4061 print all of the data for the employees' pay deductions and earnings so that pay checks may be written.

Line 4080 totals each of the withholding classifications.

Line 4100 prints a line at the bottom of the table to separate the employee data from the totals.

Line 4110 prints the totals for the Gross Pay, deductions, and Net Pay.

Line 4120 is the pause control that allows the computer operator to view the information as long as desired.

Line 4130 is the RETURN Instruction which sends the computer back to the Multiple Function Selection routine.

2. Overtime Calculations

Overtime is the first calculation that must be made because it increases the Gross Pay on which the other calculations are based. This calculation will take all of the weeks with hours over 40 and increase the pay for the overtime hours to time and a half.

Step 3.   Type In and Enter:

```
1010 REM - OVERTIME
1020 IF A(20+E)>40 THEN A(E)=A(E)+(A(20+E)−40) * (H/2)
1030 IF A(40+E)>40 THEN A(E)=A(E)+(A(40+E)−40) * (H/2)
```

Each of the calculation routines will be labeled by a REM Instruction so that a person reading the Listed program may go directly to the portion of the program desired. Line 1010 is the Remark instruction for the overtime calculation.

Lines 1020 and 1030 proceed with the calculations for the respective weeks by first determining through an IF THEN Instruction if the number of hours for a given week exceed 40.

This IF THEN Instruction uses a new computer signal which can compare two Numeric Values to determine if one is larger than another (>). The smaller value to be tested is placed on the pointed end of the signal. In other words, the first part of Line 1020 says: If the hours for Week 1 as stored in the Array A(20+E) are larger than (>) 40, proceed with the instructions in the rest of this line. If the hours do not exceed 40, the program automatically drops to the next line.

The remaining calculations to the right of the THEN in Lines 1020 and 1030 follow this sequence:

1. 40 is subtracted from the total number of hours to determine the number of overtime hours, A(20+E)-40.

2. The overtime hours are multiplied by half the normal hourly rate to determine the additional overtime pay, *(H/2)

3. This overtime pay is added to the Gross Pay.

Money in the United States is figured as dollars and cents with 100 cents to the dollar. The calculations must eliminate values less than a cent.

The computer instruction INT, which is short for Integer, will drop off any value to the right of the decimal point. Line 1040 uses this instruction to round off the Gross Pay. Level I will not round off values greater than $325 so delete Line 1040 for payrolls which will exceed this amount. Level II does not have this limitation.

Step 4.   Type In and Enter:

1040 A(E)=INT(100 * A(E)+.5)/100

The sequence of steps the calculation follows are:

1. The Gross Pay, A(E) is multiplied by 100. For example, 1.556 would become 155.6 and 1.554 would become 155.4.

2. Then .5 is added to this amount. This .5 bumps any value greater than a half penny up to the next penny. Thus, 155.6 would become 156.1 and 155.4 would become 155.9.

3. The INT Instruction drops off any value to the right of the decimal point. 156.1 becomes 156 and 155.9 becomes 155.

4. This is then divided by one hundred. 156 becomes 1.56 and 155 becomes 1.55.

3. State Disability Insurance

State Disability Insurance is the easiest deduction to determine. It is figured by multiplying the Gross Pay by one percent.

Step 5.   Type In and Enter:

1050 REM - STATE DISABILITY INSURANCE (SDI) = A(120+E)

1060 A(120+E)=A(E) * .01

1070 A(120+E)=INT(100 * A(120+E)+.5)/100

RUN

Line 1050 labels the calculation in the program. Line 1060 performs the calculation and Line 1070 rounds off the amount to the nearest cent.

4. Social Security Tax

Social Security Tax for 1979 is figured at 6.13% of the Gross Pay for all earnings under $22,900. No Social Security Tax is charged on annual wages that exceed $22,900.

The computer is not programmed to remember the earnings of each employee from the previous pay periods. Therefore, the computer operator must indicate whether or not a given employee has exceeded the taxable income. This is achieved by the Yes/No routine in Lines 1110 to 1130.

Step 6.   Type In and Enter:

```
1100 REM - SOCIAL SECURITY TAX (FICA)=A(60+E)
1110 PRINT"HAS  "; A$; "  EARNED OVER  ";
1111 A=0:Y=1:N=2:INPUT"$22,900 THIS YEAR (Y/N)"; A
1120 ON A GOTO 1140, 1150
1130 GOTO 1110
1140 A(60+E)=0:GOTO1200
1150 A(60+E)=A(E) * .0613
1160 A(60+E)=INT(100 * A(60+E)+ .5)/100
```

If the employee has earned less than this amount, the No answer sends the program to Line 1150 which figures the deduction. The Gross Pay, A(E), is multiplied by .0613 and the resulting value is assigned to the Array A(60+E). Line 1160 rounds off the Social Security withholding to the nearest cent.

If the employee has earned more than $22,900, the Yes answer sends the program to Line 1140 which sets the Social Security withholding at zero. The second instruction in Line 1140 directs the program to Line 1200 which will start the next calculation.

If no employee's wages exceed $22,900, all that is required are the lines that perform the calculation for the deduction. In this case, leave out Lines 1110 to 1140.

LEVEL II - This is the standard Level II substitution for the Yes/No decision as originally described on page 51.

Level II Substitution

```
1111 INPUT"$22,900 THIS YEAR (Y/N)"; Y$:IFY$="Y"THEN1140
1120 IF Y$="N" THEN 1150
```

5. Federal Income Tax

The procedures for computerizing Federal Income Tax deductions are not as complicated as one might expect. This is because the instructions for calculating the withholding deductions are written in a very precise sequence of steps. This is exactly the way a computer thinks. It is therefore only necessary to translate these steps into the computer's language. Shown below is an extract from page 15 of the 1979 Federal Employer's Tax Guide, Circular E.

Income Tax Withholding—Percentage Method

Percentage Method Income Tax Withholding Table

Payroll period	One with-holding allowance
Weekly	$19.23
Biweekly	38.46
Semimonthly	41.66
Monthly	83.33
Quarterly	250.00
Semiannually	500.00
Annually	1,000.00
Daily or miscellaneous (each day of the payroll period)	2.74

number of allowances the employee claims.

(b) Subtract that amount from the employee's wages.

(c) Determine amount to withhold from appropriate table on pages 16 and 17.

Use these steps to figure the income tax to withhold under the percentage method:

(a) Multiply one withholding allowance (see table above) by the

Step (a)

The first step in figuring the Federal Income Tax withholding is to multiply one withholding allowance from the table by the number of allowances the employee claims. One withholding allowance for a biweekly pay period is fixed at $38.46. The allowances claimed by the employees are stored in the Variable X. Therefore Step (a) is written: $38.46 times X.

Step (b)

This amount is then subtracted from the employee's Gross Pay, A(E), to determine the taxable income. This taxable income is stored in the Variable F, Line 121Ø.

Line 12ØØ labels the beginning of the Federal Income Tax withholding calculations.

Step 7. Type In and Enter:

```
1200 REM - FEDERAL INCOME TAX (FIT)=A(80+E)
1210 F=A(E)-(38. 46 * X)
```

Step (c)

This step determines the amount of Federal Income Tax to be withheld by using the appropriate tables on page 16 and 17 of the Employer's Tax Guide.

For this example, Table 2, shown at the bottom of the page is used to determine the deduction because it is the table for the biweekly pay period. The first part of this table is for single persons including head of the household, the other section is for married persons.

Step 8.   Type In and Enter:

```
1220 ON M GOTO 1230, 1240, 1230
1230 REM - TABLE A FOR SINGLE AND HEAD OF HOUSE
1240 REM - TABLE B FOR MARRIED PERSON
```

Line 1220 determines the Marital Status of the employee. This information is stored in the Variable M of the employee data files. Remember, 1 is single, 2 is married, and 3 is head of the household. In Line 1220, the ON Instruction takes the value in the Variable M and counts over to the appropriate Line Number in the GOTO Instruction. As indicated by the REM Instruction, Line 1230 is the beginning of the table for single persons including head of the household. Line 1240 is the beginning of the table for married persons.

The Tax Table may be almost directly translated into computer language. For example, the instruction in the first line of Tax Table 2a reads: If the amount of the wage is not over (less than) $55, the amount of the income tax to be withheld is 0. In computer language this is written: IF F < 55 THEN A(80+E)=0. F is the Variable that holds the taxable income and A(80+E) is the Array that will hold the Federal Income Tax. The entire Table 2a is translated into computer language by Lines 1231 to 1238 in Step 9.

TABLE 2. BIWEEKLY Payroll Period
(a) SINGLE person—including head of household:

If the amount of wages is: The amount of income tax to be withheld shall be:

Not over $55 0

Over—	But not over—		of excess over—
$55	—$127	15%	—$55
$127	—$262	$10.80 plus 18%	—$127
$262	—$392	$35.10 plus 21%	—$262
$392	—$546	$62.40 plus 26%	—$392
$546	—$662	$102.44 plus 30%	—$546
$662	—$865	$137.24 plus 34%	—$662
$865		$206.26 plus 39%	—$865

TABLE 2. BIWEEKLY Payroll Period

(a) SINGLE person—including head of household:

If the amount of wages is: *The amount of income tax to be withheld shall be:*

Not over $55 0

Over—	But not over—		of excess over—
$55	—$127	. . . . 15%	—$55
$127	—$262	. . . . $10.80 plus 18%	—$127
$262	—$392	. . . . $35.10 plus 21%	—$262
$392	—$546	. . . . $62.40 plus 26%	—$392
$546	—$662	. . . $102.44 plus 30%	—$546
$662	—$865	. . . $137.24 plus 34%	—$662
$865	. . . .	$206.26 plus 39%	—$865

Step 9. Type In and Enter:

```
1231 IF F<55 THEN A(80+E)=0:GOTO1250
1232 IF F<127 THEN A(80+E)=.15 * (F−55):GOTO1250
1233 IF F<262 THEN A(80+E)=10. 80+. 18 * (F−127):GOTO1250
1234 IF F<392 THEN A(80+E)=35. 10+. 21 * (F−262):GOTO1250
1235 IF F<546 THEN A(80+E)=62. 40+. 26 * (F−392):GOTO1250
1236 IF F<662 THEN A(80+E)=102. 44+. 30 * (F−546):GOTO1250
1237 IF F<865 THEN A(80+E)=137. 24+. 34 * (F−662):GOTO1250
1238 A(80+E)=202. 26+. 39 * (F−865):GOTO1250
1250 A(80+E)=INT(100 * A(80+E)+.5)/100
```

To further see how this translation of the Tax Tables is read by the computer, take as an example a single person who has earned $233 in a pay period.

The program will proceed from Line 1220 to Line 1230 because the person is single. Line 1230 is a REM Instruction so the program goes to Line 1231. Line 1231 asks if F is less than $55. It is not, so the program goes to Line 1232. This line asks if F is less than $127. It is not, so the program goes to Line 1233. This line asks if F is less than $262. It is, so the program proceeds to the instructions to the right of the THEN Instruction in Line 1233. A(80+E), the Federal Income Tax, is calculated to be $10.80 plus 18% of the taxable income over $127, F minus 127. From here, the program proceeds to Line 1250 which is the line that rounds off the Federal Income Tax withholding.

Lines 1241 to 1248 translate Table 2b just as Lines 1231 to 1238 translate Table 2a.

TABLE 2. BIWEEKLY Payroll Period

(b) MARRIED person—

If the amount of wages is:		The amount of income tax to be withheld shall be:	
Not over $92 0			

Over—	But not over—		of excess over—
$92	—$254	.... 15%	—$92
$254	—$419	.... $24.30 plus 18%	—$254
$419	—$577	.... $54.00 plus 21%	—$419
$577	—$738	.... $87.18 plus 24%	—$577
$738	—$908	.... $125.82 plus 28%	—$738
$908	—$1,112	.... $173.42 plus 32%	—$908
$1,112	....	$238.70 plus 37%	—$1,112

Step 10.   Type In and Enter:

```
1241 IF F<92 THEN A(80+E)=0:GOTO1250
1242 IF F<254 THEN A(80+E)=.15 * (F−92):GOTO1250
1243 IF F<419 THEN A(80+E)=24. 30+. 18 * (F−254):GOTO1250
1244 IF F<577 THEN A(80+E)=54. 00+. 21 * (F−419):GOTO1250
1245 IF F<738 THEN A(80+E)=87. 18+. 24 * (F−577):GOTO1250
1246 IF F<908 THEN A(80+E)=125. 82+. 28 * (F−738):GOTO1250
1247 IF F<1112 THEN A(80+E)=173. 42+. 32 * (F−908):GOTO1250
1248 A(80+E)=238. 70+. 37 * (F−1112)
RUN
```

6. State Income Tax

The California State Income Tax withholding calculations are more involved than the Federal Income Tax because there are five tables to translate instead of just one. Fortunately, it is not any harder to translate the California Tax Tables because they are written with the same precise sequence of logical steps. If the reader does not need this information, this sequence of lines may be left out and the program will run fine.

The steps for calculating the California State Income Tax withholding (by the exact calculation method) are listed on page 37 of the 1979 Employer's Tax Guide. There are five steps, one for each of the tax tables. These steps will be extracted and reproduced just prior to the description and program lines which will translate them into computer language.

METHOD B — EXACT CALCULATION METHOD

This method is based upon applying a given percentage to the wages (after deductions) which fall within a taxable income class, adding to this product the given accumulated tax for all lower tax brackets, and then subtracting a tax credit based on the number of allowances claimed on the employee's Withholding Allowance Certificate (California Form DE-4 or Federal Form W-4). This method also takes into consideration the special treatment of additional allowances for itemized deductions (see pages 15 and 16).

The steps in computing the amount of tax to be withheld are as follows:

Step (1)   Determine if the employee's gross salaries and wages are less than or equal to the amount shown in Table A - Low Income Exemption Table. If so, no income tax is required to be withheld.

TABLE A - Low Income Exemption Table

Payroll Period	Single	Married Allowances on DE-4 or W-4 "0" or "1"	Married Allowances on DE-4 or W-4 "2" or more	Head of Household
Weekly	$96.15	$96.15	$192.31	$192.31
Biweekly	192.31	192.31	384.62	384.62
Semimonthly	208.33	208.33	416.67	416.67
Monthly	416.67	416.67	833.33	833.33
Quarterly	1,250.00	1,250.00	2,500.00	2,500.00
Semiannual	2,500.00	2,500.00	5,000.00	5,000.00
Annual	5,000.00	5,000.00	10,000.00	10,000.00
Daily or misc.	13.70	13.70	27.40	27.40

Table A lists the incomes from which no taxes are withheld. The biweekly pay period shows $192.31 to be the lowest taxable income for single persons and married persons with less than two exemptions (one or none). $384.62 is the lowest taxable income for married persons with two or more exemptions and head of households.

This table uses the information in two of the Variables from the employee data files. M is the Variable for Marital Status and X is the Variable for the number of Tax Exemptions.

Step 11.   Type In and Enter:

```
1300 REM - STATE INCOME TAX (SIT)=A(100+E)
1310 ON M GOTO 1320, 1340, 1350
1320 IF A(E)<192.31 THEN A(100+E)=0:GOTO1590
1330 GOTO 1400
1340 IF X<2 THEN 1320
1350 IF A(E)<384.62 THEN A(100+E)=0:GOTO1590
```

If a person is single (M=1), then the program will go to Line 1320. If the wages are less than $192.31, the state withholding is set at zero and the program proceeds to Line 1590 which is the end of the state tax calculations.

If a person is a head of household (M=3), the program will go to Line 1350. This line determines if the wages are less than $384.62. If the wages are less than this, the state withholding is set at zero and the program progresses to the end of the state tax calculations, Line 159Ø. If the wages are more than $384.62, then the program drops down to the next line which is 14ØØ.

For married persons (M=2), the program is sent to Line 134Ø. This line determines the number of tax exemptions from the Variable X. If there are less than two exemptions, the program is sent to Line 132Ø where the wages are checked as they were for single persons. If there are two or more exemptions, the program is sent to Line 135Ø where the minimum taxable wage is $384.62.

---

(2)   If the employee claims additional withholding allowances for itemized deductions, subtract the employee's itemized deduction allowance shown in <u>Table B - Itemized Deduction Allowance Table</u> from the gross salaries and wages.

Step 2 allows employees to declare special exemptions for deductible expenses. This step is deferred to the Appendix because many California businesses do not use this provision. It also requires rewriting all of the READ and DATA Lines to add the extra exemption classification.

---

(3)   Subtract the employee's standard deduction shown in <u>Table C - Standard Deduction Table</u>* to arrive at the employee's taxable income.

TABLE C - Standard Deduction Table

Payroll period	Single	Married — Allowances on DE-4 or W-4 "0" or "1"	Married — Allowances on DE-4 or W-4 "2" or more	Head of Household
Weekly	$19.23	$19.23	$38.46	$38.46
Biweekly	38.46	38.46	76.92	76.92
Semimonthly	41.67	41.67	83.33	83.33
Monthly	83.33	83.33	166.67	166.67
Quarterly	250.00	250.00	500.00	500.00
Semiannual	500.00	500.00	1,000.00	1,000.00
Annual	1,000.00	1,000.00	2,000.00	2,000.00
Daily or misc.	2.74	2.74	5.48	5.48

Step 3 figures the taxable income of the employee by subtracting the fixed amount of either $38.46 or $76.92 from the employee's Gross Pay. The specific amount to be subtracted is determined by the marital status and number of tax exemptions. Therefore, Lines 14ØØ to 143Ø function the same as Lines 131Ø to 135Ø which were just described on the previous page. The taxable income for the state is stored in the Variable S.

Step 12.   Type In and Enter:

```
1400 ON M GOTO 1410, 1420, 1430
1410 S=A(E)−38. 46:GOTO1450
1420 IF X<2 THEN 1410
1430 S=A(E)−76. 92
```

(4) Use <u>Table E - Tax Rate Table</u> for the payroll period to find the applicable line on which the taxable income is located. Perform the indicated calculation to arrive at the computed tax.

Tax Table E is the same type of table that was used to determine the Federal Income Tax deduction. Line 1450 selects the appropriate table using the Marital Status of the employee. The individual tables are translated into computer language the same way the Federal Tax Tables were translated (pages 77 and 78). Line 1520 in the GOTO Instructions is the beginning of the next calculation for the state tax.

Step 13.   Type In and Enter:

1450 ON M GOTO 1460, 1480, 1500

1460 REM - SINGLE PERSON TAX TABLE

1480 REM - MARRIED PERSON TAX TABLE

1500 REM - HEAD OF HOUSE TAX TABLE

(A)   SINGLE Person

If the taxable income is:

At least–	But less than–	Computed tax is:		Of amount over–
$1	$81......		1%	$1
81	142......	$.80 plus	2%	81
142	202......	2.00 plus	3%	142
202	263......	3.80 plus	4%	202
263	324......	6.30 plus	5%	263
324	385......	9.30 plus	6%	324
385	445......	13.00 plus	7%	385
445	506......	17.20 plus	8%	445
506	567......	22.10 plus	9%	506
567	627......	27.50 plus	10%	567
627 and over.........		33.60 plus	11%	627

Step 14.   Type In and Enter:

1461 IF S<81 THEN A(100+E)=.01 ✳ S:GOTO1520

1462 IF S<142 THEN A(100+E)=.80+.02 ✳ (S−81):GOTO1520

1463 IF S<202 THEN A(100+E)=2.00+.03 ✳ (S−142):GOTO1520

1464 IF S<263 THEN A(100+E)=3.80+.04 ✳ (S−202):GOTO1520

1465 IF S<324 THEN A(100+E)=6.30+.05 ✳ (S−263):GOTO1520

1466 IF S<385 THEN A(100+E)=9.30+.06 ✳ (S−324):GOTO1520

1467 IF S<445 THEN A(100+E)=13.00+.07 ✳ (S−385):GOTO1520

1468 IF S<506 THEN A(100+E)=17.20+.08 ✳ (S−445):GOTO1520

1469 IF S<567 THEN A(100+E)=22.10+.09 ✳ (S−506):GOTO1520

1470 IF S<627 THEN A(100+E)=27.50+.10 ✳ (S−567):GOTO1520

1471 A(100+E)=33.60+.11 ✳ (S−627):GOTO1520

(B) MARRIED Person

If the taxable income is:

At least-	But less than-	Computed tax is:		Of amount over-
$1	$162......		1%	$1
162	284......	$1.60 plus	2%	162
284	404......	4.00 plus	3%	284
404	526......	7.60 plus	4%	404
526	648......	12.60 plus	5%	526
648	770......	18.60 plus	6%	648
770	890......	26.00 plus	7%	770
890	1,012......	34.40 plus	8%	890
1,012	1,134......	44.20 plus	9%	1,012
1,134	1,254......	55.00 plus	10%	1,134
1,254 and over.........		67.20 plus	11%	1,254

(C) HEAD OF HOUSEHOLD

If the taxable income is:

At least-	But less than-	Computed tax is:		Of amount over-
$1	$162......		1%	$1
162	243......	$1.60 plus	2%	162
243	303......	3.20 plus	3%	243
303	364......	5.10 plus	4%	303
364	425......	7.50 plus	5%	364
425	486......	10.50 plus	6%	425
486	546......	14.20 plus	7%	486
546	607......	18.40 plus	8%	546
607	668......	23.30 plus	9%	607
668	728......	28.70 plus	10%	668
728 and over.........		34.80 plus	11%	728

Step 15. Type In and Enter:

```
1481 IF S<162 THEN A(100+E)=.01 * S:GOTO1520
1482 IF S<284 THEN A(100+E)=1.60+.02 * (S-162):GOTO1520
1483 IF S<404 THEN A(100+E)=4.00+.03 * (S-284):GOTO1520
1484 IF S<526 THEN A(100+E)=7.60+.04 * (S-404):GOTO1520
1485 IF S<648 THEN A(100+E)=12.60+.05 * (S-526):GOTO1520
1486 IF S<770 THEN A(100+E)=18.60+.06 * (S-648):GOTO1520
1487 IF S<890 THEN A(100+E)=26.00+.07 * (S-770):GOTO1520
1488 IF S<1012 THEN A(100+E)=34.40+.08 * (S-890):GOTO1520
1489 IF S<1134 THEN A(100+E)=44.20+.09 * (S-1012):GOTO1520
1490 IF S<1254 THEN A(100+E)=55.00+.10 * (S-1134):GOTO1520
1491 A(100+E)=67.20+.11 * (S-1254):GOTO1520
```

Step 16. Type In and Enter:

```
1501 IF S<162 THEN A(100+E)=.01 * S:GOTO1520
1502 IF S<243 THEN A(100+E)=1.60+.02 * (S-162):GOTO1520
1503 IF S<303 THEN A(100+E)=3.20+.03 * (S-243):GOTO1520
1504 IF S<364 THEN A(100+E)=5.10+.04 * (S-303):GOTO1520
1505 IF S<425 THEN A(100+E)=7.50+.05 * (S-364):GOTO1520
1506 IF S<486 THEN A(100+E)=10.50+.06 * (S-425):GOTO1520
1507 IF S<546 THEN A(100+E)=14.20+.07 * (S-486):GOTO1520
1508 IF S<607 THEN A(100+E)=18.40+.08 * (S-546):GOTO1520
1509 IF S<668 THEN A(100+E)=23.30+.09 * (S-607):GOTO1520
1510 IF S<728 THEN A(100+E)=28.70+.10 * (S-668):GOTO1520
1511 A(100+E)=34.80+.11 * (S-728):GOTO1520
```

TABLE D - Tax Credit Table

Payroll period	Marital status	Allowances on DE-4 or W-4									
		0	1	2	3	4	5	6	7	8	9	10 or more+
Weekly	Single	0	$.48	$.63	$.79	$.94	$1.10	$1.25	$1.40	$1.56	$1.71	$1.87
	Other*	0	.48	.96	1.12	1.27	1.42	1.58	1.73	1.88	2.04	2.19
Biweekly	Single	0	.96	1.27	1.58	1.88	2.19	2.50	2.81	3.12	3.42	3.73
	Other*	0	.96	1.92	2.23	2.54	2.85	3.15	3.46	3.77	4.08	4.38
Semimonthly	Single	0	1.04	1.38	1.71	2.04	2.38	2.71	3.04	3.38	3.71	4.04
	Other*	0	1.04	2.08	2.42	2.75	3.08	3.42	3.75	4.08	4.42	4.75

* Married or Head of Household.

+ If the number of allowances claimed exceeds 10, you may determine the amount of tax credit to be allowed by multiplying the difference between the amounts shown for 9 and "10 or more" allowances by the number of allowances claimed in excess of 10 and then adding to this product the amount shown for "10 or more" allowances.

Step 5 subtracts a tax credit from the computed tax to arrive at the final amount to be withheld. Once again, this table is based both on the marital status and tax exemptions claimed by the employees.

Step 17.   Type In and Enter:

```
1520 ON M GOTO 1530, 1550, 1550
1530 REM - SINGLE TAX TABLE
1550 REM - OTHER TAX TABLE
```

Line 1520 determines the Marital Status from the Variable M and directs the program to the appropriate table. The titles of the two tables are established by the REM Instructions in Lines 1530 and 1550.

Step 18.   Type In and Enter:

```
1531 IF X=0 THEN 1590
1532 ON X GOTO 1535, 1536, 1537, 1538, 1539, 1540, 1541, 1542, 1543, 1544
1533 GOTO 1544
1551 IF X=0 THEN 1590
1552 ON X GOTO 1555, 1556, 1557, 1558, 1559, 1560, 1561, 1562, 1563, 1564
1553 GOTO 1564
1590 A(100+E)=INT(100 * A(100+E)+.5)/100
```

Lines 1531 to 1533 and Lines 1551 to 1553 use the Tax Exemption as stored in the Variable X to direct the program to the Line Number that will deduct the appropriate Tax Credit.

If X is zero, then no tax credit is given so the program goes to Line 1590, the end of the state tax routine.

If X is between 1 and 10, the ON GOTO Instruction in Lines 1532 or 1552 counts over to the Line Number which will make the appropriate deduction from the state tax. For example, if a single person claims two exemptions, the ON Instruction of Line 1532 will count over to the second Line Number in the GOTO Instruction and direct the program to Line 1536.

If X is greater than 10, the program drops down to Line 1533 or 1553. These two lines send the program to the last line of their respective tax tables, Lines 1544 and 1564.

Line 1590 is the last line for the state tax calculations. It rounds off the income tax withholding to the nearest cent.

Step 19.   Type In and Enter:

```
1535 A(100+E)=A(100+E)−.96:GOTO1590
1536 A(100+E)=A(100+E)−1.27:GOTO1590
1537 A(100+E)=A(100+E)−1.58:GOTO1590
1538 A(100+E)=A(100+E)−1.88:GOTO1590
1539 A(100+E)=A(100+E)−2.19:GOTO1590
1540 A(100+E)=A(100+E)−2.50:GOTO1590
1541 A(100+E)=A(100+E)−2.81:GOTO1590
1542 A(100+E)=A(100+E)−3.12:GOTO1590
1543 A(100+E)=A(100+E)−3.42:GOTO1590
1544 A(100+E)=A(100+E)−(3.73+(X−10)*.31):GOTO1590
```

Lines 1535 through 1543 subtract the appropriate Tax Credit from the State Income Tax withholding and send the program to Line 1590.

Line 1544 determines the tax credit for 10 or more exemptions. This tax credit is $3.73 plus .31 times the number of exemptions over ten.

Step 20, on the next page, translates the lower half of the biweekly Tax Credit Table.

```
1555 A(100+E)=A(100+E)-.96:GOTO1590
1556 A(100+E)=A(100+E)-1.92:GOTO1590
1557 A(100+E)=A(100+E)-2.23:GOTO1590
1558 A(100+E)=A(100+E)-2.54:GOTO1590
1559 A(100+E)=A(100+E)-2.85:GOTO1590
1560 A(100+E)=A(100+E)-3.15:GOTO1590
1561 A(100+E)=A(100+E)-3.46:GOTO1590
1562 A(100+E)=A(100+E)-3.77:GOTO1590
1563 A(100+E)=A(100+E)-4.08:GOTO1590
1564 A(100+E)=A(100+E)-(4.38+(X-10)*.30)
```

7. Net Pay

The Net Pay is calculated by subtracting the deductions from the Gross Pay.

Step 21.   Type In and Enter:

```
1600 REM - NET PAY =A(140+E)
1610 A(140+E)=A(E)-A(60+E)-A(80+E)-A(100+E)-A(120+E)
```

8. Expanding the Information Storage

The program lines which store and retrieve information on cassette tapes must be expanded to include the payroll deductions. The PRINT # Instructions which store information were described on page 65 and the INPUT # Instructions were described on page 68.

Step 22.   Type In and Enter:

```
5040 IF C=-1 THENA(E)=0:A(60+E)=0:A(80+E)=0:A(100+E)=0:A(120+E)=0
5060 PRINT#A(E);",";A(80+E);",";A(60+E);",";A(100+E);",";A(120+E)
6090 INPUT# A(E), A(80+E), A(60+E), A(100+E),  A(120+E)
```

Level II Substitution

```
5060 PRINT#-1, A(E), A(80+E), A(60+E), A(100+E), A(120+E)
6090 INPUT#-1, A(E), A(80+E), A(60+E), A(100+E), A(120+E)
```

The Totaling Program

Totaling programs are used to add together information that has been created by several runs of a given program, such as the Payroll Program. Totaling Programs start by retrieving the information that has been stored on the cassette tape. This information is then displayed in various formats and totaled.

The Payroll Totaling Program described here is comprised of three parts. The first part is a retrieval routine which recovers the information that has been stored on the cassette tape. The second section of the program then displays this information by employee. The pay records for the first employee are displayed and totaled, then the records for the second employee are displayed and totaled, etc. After the pay records for all of the employees have been displayed, the third part of this program displays the totals of each of the employees. This information is added together as it is displayed so that the total for all the employees' wages and deductions may be seen. These totals may be used to prepare expense records and tax statements.

The main consideration for a totaling program is that a vast amount of information has to be handled. This requires an extensive use of Arrays. For example, in the Payroll Program there were five pieces of data stored for each employee for a given pay period (the Gross Pay and four deductions). The program is written to handle up to 2Ø employees for a total of 1ØØ pieces of data in a given pay period. At the end of the year, there are 26 biweekly pay periods with 26ØØ pieces of data.

Radio Shack's Level I has only one Array to hold all of this information, A( ). The basic data will be broken down into five groups within this Array.

Name	Abbreviation	Array	Level II
Gross Pay		A(E)	GP(E, J)
Federal Income Tax	FIT	A(2Ø+E)	FT(E, J)
Social Security Tax	FICA	A(4Ø+E)	SS(E, J)
State Income Tax	SIT	A(6Ø+E)	ST(E, J)
State Disability Insurance	SDI	A(8Ø+E)	SD(E, J)

The names of these Arrays are different from the names of the Arrays used for this same information in the Payroll Program. This does not matter because the cassette tape does not remember names, only data.

To make a distinction between the different pay periods, 1ØØ is added to the Numeric Value in the Array name. In other words, A(E+1ØØ) is the Gross Pay for the first pay period and A(E+2ØØ) is the Gross Pay for the second pay period. A(2Ø+E+1ØØ) is the Federal Income Tax for the first pay period, etc.

The Array from A(1) to A(1ØØ) is reserved to hold the totals for each employee's pay record.

Level II users may also wish to change the names of the Arrays. This is not an essential substitution to make the program run properly so it will be left to the reader to make the necessary changes. The table on page 87 suggests some Arrays for Level II that are two dimensional. The Gross Pay, for example, is stored in GP(E, J) where E is the dimension that remembers the Employee Number and J is the dimension that remembers the pay period.

1. Retrieving Information

The Payroll Totaling Program is a new program. The Payroll Program will have to be dumped from the computer's memory by a NEW Instruction before the Totaling Program can be entered. Make sure the Payroll Program has been recorded on a cassette tape.

The routine for retrieving the information from the cassette tape has the same basic lines as those that were described in the Payroll Program. Therefore, the program lines in Step 1 below are the same instructions that were described on pages 68 to 70.

Step 1.   Type In and Enter:

```
NEW
2000 CLS:PRINT"PREPARE TO RETRIEVE PAYROLL"
2010 INPUT"IS THE TAPE RECORDER IN PLAY (Y)"; A
2040 INPUT # B, D, W
2050 PRINT"THIS PAY PERIOD STARTS"; B;" AND ENDS"; D
2070 INPUT"RETRIEVE:1. THIS PAY PERIOD, 2. ANOTHER"; A
2080 ON A GOTO 2100, 2040
2090 GOTO 2070
2100 FOR I=1 TO W
2110 INPUT # E
2130 INPUT # A(E), A(20+E), A(40+E), A(60+E), A(80+E)
2140 NEXT I
2160 PRINT"THE PAYROLL IS RETRIEVED"
```

LEVEL II - A DIM Instruction must be used to tell the computer how many Variables are going to be used in the Array A( ). If this is not done, an error message will occur.

Information is retrieved from the cassette tape in Level II by using the computer instruction INPUT #-1.

```
Level II Substitution

10 DIM A(2700)
2040 INPUT # −1, B, D, W
2110  INPUT # −1, E
2130  INPUT # −1, A(E), A(20+E), A(40+E), A(60+E), A(80+E)
```

This retrieval process will be repeated for each of the pay periods that have been recorded. The computer operator must tell the program how many pay periods have been recorded. This information is stored in the Variable K.

Step 2.   Type In and Enter:

```
2020 INPUT"NUMBER OF PAY PERIODS TO RETRIEVE"; K
```

A FOR NEXT Loop is used to repeat the retrieval routine for the number of pay periods indicated. The entire retrieval routine from Line 2040 to Line 2140 is repeated.

Step 3.   Type In and Enter:

```
2030 FOR J=1 TO K
2150 NEXT J
```

The Numeric Value in the name of the Array must be stepped up by 100 each time another pay period is recovered because each pay period may use up to 100 Variables. The Employee Number is first retrieved by Line 2110. Then the number of the pay period being retrieved, J, is multiplied by 100. This is added to the Employee Number to create the Employee Number for the pay period being retrieved.

Step 4.   Type In and Enter:

```
2120 E=J * 100+E
```

Each time the FOR NEXT Loop completes a pass through the program, the value of J is increased in value by 1.

As a result of this process, the first employee's new Employee Number for the first pay period is 1∅1, for the second period it is 2∅1, etc. This new Employee Number is then used to determine the specific name of each Array. The Gross Pay, A(E), for the first employee's first pay period is A(1∅1) and for the second pay period it is A(2∅1). The Federal Income Tax, A(2∅+E), for the first employee's first pay period is A(121), for the second pay period it is A(221), etc.

Lines 2∅7∅ to 2∅9∅ (see Step 1) are used to make sure the tape recorder is starting to pick up the data from the correct pay period. These steps are used only for the first pay period. After this the pay periods are automatically picked up from their subsequent locations on the tape. Therefore, Line 2∅6∅ bypasses Lines 2∅7∅ through 2∅9∅ after the correct starting location has been found.

Step 5. Type In and Enter:

```
2060 IF J>1 THEN 2100
```

The value of J is 1 during the first pass of the FOR NEXT Loop. After this, the value of J is increased by 1 for each subsequent pass. When J is greater than 1, the program is directed to jump over Lines 2∅7∅ to 2∅9∅ by Line 2∅6∅.

2. Displaying Individual Employee Records

Each employee's pay records are displayed one at a time on the Video Screen in a table which lists Gross Pay, the deductions, and Net Pay for each pay period.

The first step is to create DATA Instructions which hold the Employee Number and the Employee Name, Lines 251∅ to 253∅. A READ Instruction is established in Line 3∅3∅. Notice that the Employee Number is read by the Variable G instead of the Variable E. This is because the Variable E has been changed to store the Employee Number by pay period. The String Variable A$ is still used for the Employee Name.

Step 6. Type In and Enter:

```
2500 REM - EMPLOYEE RECORDS
2510 DATA 1, HARRISON
2520 DATA 2, SAMUELS
2530 DATA 3, JOHNSON
3030 READ G, A$
```

The format for the display of the employees' pay records is established by the following PRINT and TAB instructions.

Step 7. Type In and Enter:

```
3050 CLS:PRINT TAB(20); A$; "'S PAYROLL RECORDS"
3060 PRINT:PRINT"PAY PERIOD"; TAB(15); "GROSS"; TAB(26); "FIT";
3061 PRINT TAB(34); "FICA"; TAB(41); "SIT"; TAB(48); "SDI"; TAB(55); "NET"
3090 PRINT TAB(5); J; TAB(14); A(E); TAB(25); A(20+E); TAB(33);
3091 PRINT A(40+E); TAB (40); A(60+E); TAB(47); A(80+E); TAB(54); F
RUN 2500
```

Step 8. The Computer Will Print:

HARRISON'S PAYROLL RECORDS

PAY PERIOD	GROSS	FIT	FICA	SIT	SDI	NET
0	0	0	0	0	0	0

Line 3050 sets up the title of the table by incorporating the Employee's Name, as retrieved by the Variable A$ from the DATA Instruction, with the fixed information inside the quotation marks.

Lines 3060 and 3061 create the headings for the columns and Lines 3090 and 3091 print the information from the Arrays in the appropriate columns.

The information about the Net Pay was not stored on the cassette tape. Therefore, the Net Pay is recalculated by subtracting the withholding information from the Gross Pay. This is then stored in the Variable F.

Step 9. Type In and Enter:

```
3080 F=A(E)-A(20+E)-A(40+E)-A(60+E)-A(80+E)
```

All of the information from the cassette tape may be recovered by this program from the first pay period of the year to the last. In some cases it may be desirable to see only a limited amount of this information. For example, in midyear perhaps only the pay periods for the last quarter are to be displayed. Line 3000 gives the computer operator the option of selecting which portion of the information will be displayed.

Step 10.   Type In and Enter:

3000 RESTORE:INPUT"DISPLAY AND TOTAL RECORDS STARTING PAY
PERIOD #"; B
3010 IF B>K THEN 3000

Line 3010 is a safety check. K is the Variable that stores the total number of pay periods that have been retrieved from the tape. If the value of the beginning pay period entered into B is greater than the number of pay periods retrieved, the program will loop back to Line 3000. The program will not progress beyond this point until the operator makes a valid selection for B.

A FOR NEXT Loop must be placed around the instructions that print the values in the Arrays so that all of the pay periods desired at a given time may be printed. This FOR NEXT Loop is going to use a new computer instruction, STEP. Remember, each pay period is separated by 100. To read the records of the first employee, for example, the program must count 101, 201, 301, 401, etc. The STEP Instruction tells the computer the interval the computer is to use.

Step 11.   Type In and Enter:

3070 FOR E=(B ✳ 100+G) TO (K ✳ 100+G) STEP 100
3170 NEXT E

The FOR NEXT Loop starts counting at B*100+G where B is the number of the first pay period that is to be displayed (Line 3000 in Step 9), 100 is the interval between pay periods, and G is the Employee Number from the READ Instruction.

The FOR NEXT Loop counts up to K*100+G where K is the last pay period retrieved (Line 2020 in Step 2), 100 is the interval between pay periods, and G is the Employee Number.

For example, if there are 5 pay periods retrieved by K, and the program is to start from the second pay period, B, and the first employee is being processed, G, the program counts 201, 301, 401, 501.

The Variable J was used to assign a number to the pay periods as they were being retrieved from the tape ($2\emptyset 3\emptyset$ FOR J=1 TO K). For each pay period being processed, the value of J was increased by 1. J is not the Variable of the FOR NEXT Loop in the display routine. However, it is still necessary to increase the value of J by one during each pass of the FOR NEXT Loop so that each pay period will be labeled by the correct number. This is achieved by Line $31\emptyset\emptyset$ below. The first pay period to be displayed is determined by the operator placing the desired number in the Variable B, Line $3\emptyset\emptyset\emptyset$. Therefore, J must be adjusted to this value, Line $3\emptyset 4\emptyset$.

Step 12.   Type In and Enter:

```
3040 J=B
3100 J=J+1
```

Notice the initial value of J is established before the FOR NEXT Loop begins, Line $3\emptyset 4\emptyset$. The current value of J is then printed by Line $3\emptyset 9\emptyset$ (Step 7). Line $31\emptyset\emptyset$ increases the value of J by one.

Only 16 lines of information can be displayed on the Video Screen at one time. The title and the heading for the columns take up three of these lines. But by the end of the year there will be 26 lines of information that can be displayed (26 biweekly pay periods). Therefore, this program is designed to print only $1\emptyset$ lines of information at a time.

To achieve this, a counting device must be introduced into the FOR NEXT Loop, Line $31\emptyset 1$. The initial value of the counting device must be set at one before the FOR NEXT Loop starts, Line $3\emptyset 41$. This is similar to the counting that is done in the Variable J.

Step 13.   Type In and Enter:

```
3041 D=1
3101 D=D+1
```

After ten lines have been displayed on the Video Screen, the program must be sent to a pause control so that the computer operator may view the information for as long as desired.

```
3120 IF D=10 THEN 3140
3130 GOTO 3170
3140 D=1:PRINT:PRINT:INPUT"CONTINUE (Y)"; A
```

Line 3120 determines if D has reached 10. If D has not reach-ed 10, the program drops to Line 3130 which directs the program to the end of the FOR NEXT Loop, Line 3170, so that the next pay period may be printed. If D has reached 10, the program is sent to the pause control created by the INPUT Instruction in Line 3140. Notice that Line 3140 sets the value of D back to 1 so that the counting may start all over again.

LEVEL II - The Y may be dropped because it is not necessary to press anything other than the Enter Key for a Level II INPUT Instruction.

Level II Substitution

```
3140 D=1:PRINT:PRINT:INPUT"CONTINUE"; A
```

After the operator has had a chance to view the information on the screen, the program will proceed to the next set of pay periods. First, however, the Video Screen must be cleared of the existing information and the column headings must be reprinted.

```
3150 CLS:PRINT TAB(20); A$; "'S PAYROLL RECORDS"
3160 PRINT:PRINT"PAY PERIOD"; TAB(15); "GROSS"; TAB(26); "FIT";
3161 PRINT TAB(34); "FICA"; TAB(41); "SIT"; TAB(48); "SDI"; TAB(55);
"NET"
```

The program may now proceed to display the next 10 lines of information which will contain the next ten pay periods.

After all of the information for a given employee has been displayed, the program must progress to the next employee. This is achieved by putting the display routine just described into a large FOR NEXT Loop that will proceed from one employee to the next.

```
3020 FOR I=1 TO W
3200 INPUT"CONTINUE (Y)"; A
3210 NEXT I
```

Level II Substitution

```
3200 INPUT"CONTINUE"; A
```

Line 3020 establishes a FOR NEXT Loop based on the number of employees as determined by the Variable W. The value of W has been retrieved from the cassette tape in Line 2040 at the beginning of this program. Each time a new pay period is processed, a new value is assigned to this Variable. This means that the value of W is the value from the last pay period retrieved. This insures that all employees will be displayed.

Line 3200 is a pause control which allows the computer operator the chance to view the totals of an employee's records before the next employee is displayed.

3. Totaling Employee Pay Records

As the information is being displayed, it may also be totaled. The totals for each employee will be held in the Arrays A(G), A(20+G), A(40+G), A(60+G), and A(80+G). Remember, the individual records for each pay period are held in the Array from A(101) to A(2699). This leaves the Array from A(1) to A(100) open to store the totals.

The Variable G holds the Employee Number from the DATA Instructions. In this example, the Employee Numbers in these instructions are 1, 2, and 3. Therefore, A(1) will hold the Total Gross Pay for the first employee and A(21) will hold the Total Federal Income Tax for the first employee, etc.

Step 17.   Type In and Enter:

```
3042  A(G)=0:A(20+G)=0:A(40+G)=0:A(60+G)=0:A(80+G)=0:H=0
3110 A(G)=A(G)+A(E):A(20+G)=A(20+G)+A(20+E):A(40+G)=A(40+G)+A(40
+E)
3111 A(60+G)=A(60+G)+A(60+E):A(80+G)=A(80+G)+A(80+E):H=H+F
3180 PRINT TAB(15); "------------------------------"
3190 PRINT TAB(14); A(G); TAB(25); A(20+G); TAB(33); A(40+G);
3191 PRINT TAB(40); A(60+G); TAB(47); A(80+G); TAB(54); H
```

Totaling, as described earlier, is the process of first setting the Arrays at zero (Line 3042), adding the individual amounts into the totaling Array (Lines 3110 and 3111), then displaying the totals on the Video Screen under the appropriate column headings (Lines 3180, 3190, and 3191). The Variable H is used to store the Net Pay Total as derived from the individual Net Pay amounts stored in the Variable F.

One additional factor must be taken into consideration in the Totaling Program. Radio Shack's Level I does not automatically zero out the Arrays when the computer is turned on. An employee who is hired midyear will have no values assigned to the Arrays for the first part of the year. However, the computer will assign arbitrary values in these Arrays and this information will be figured into the program as the totaling is done. Therefore, an instruction must be written early in the program to zero out the Arrays before information is retrieved from the cassette tape. Lines 20 and 40 set up a FOR NEXT Loop that will pass through all of the 2700 Variables that may be used in the Array A(E). Each of these Variables is assigned an initial value of zero by Line 30. While this FOR NEXT Loop is working, the computer will not respond to information typed on the keyboard. Line 10 alerts the operator to this fact.

Step 18.   Type In and Enter:

```
10 CLS:PRINT "DO NOT DISTURB, I'M WORKING"
20 FOR E =1 TO 2700
30 A(E)=0
40 NEXT E
```

LEVEL II - These lines are not required in Level II because all Arrays and Variables are automatically zeroed out by the computer.

---

4. Displaying the Total Payroll

The last routine of this program displays the totals for each employee's wages and withholdings. This information is added together to derive the total payroll expense. This display and totaling routine is identical to the routine used in the regular Payroll Program in Lines 4000 to 4110 (see pages 72 to 73). The only change is the names of the Arrays.

```
4000 CLS: RESTORE:PRINT TAB(25); "TOTAL PAYROLL":PRINT
4010 PRINT"#"; TAB(5); "NAME"; TAB(18); "GROSS"; TAB(28); "FIT";
4011 PRINT TAB(36); "FICA"; TAB(43); "SIT"; TAB(49); "SDI"; TAB(56);
"NET"
4020 T=0:U=0:V=0:P=0:L=0
4030 FOR I=1 TO W
4040 READ G, A$
4050 PRINT G; TAB(5); A$; TAB(17); A(G); TAB(27); A(20+G); TAB(35);
4051 PRINT A(40+G); TAB(42); A(60+G); TAB(48); A(80+G);
4052 PRINT TAB(55); A(G)−A(20+G)−A(40+G)−A(60+G)−A(80+G)
4060 T=T+A(G):U=U+A(20+G):V=V+A(40+G):P=P+A(60+G):L=L+A(80
+G)
4070 NEXT I
4080 PRINT TAB(20); "− − − − − − − − − − − − − − − − − − − − − − − − − −"
4090 PRINT TAB(17); T; TAB(27); U; TAB(35); V; TAB(42); P; TAB(48); L
```

After the payroll is totaled, the employer's contribution to Social Security is displayed by Line 4100. Employers match the amount withheld from the employee's pay checks with a similar amount. The total amount withheld from the employee's pay checks is stored in the Variable V. Therefore, this Variable may be used to indicate the employer's expense.

The employer's Unemployment Insurance expense is displayed by Line 4110. In California, this expense varies from employer to employer depending on the turnover of the particular business. In this example, the Unemployment Insurance is shown as 2.5% of the Total Gross Wages. The Total Gross Wages are stored in the Variable T.

```
4100 PRINT:PRINT"EMPLOYER'S FICA EXPENSE"; V
4110 PRINT"UNEMPLOYMENT INSURANCE EXPENSE"; INT(2.5 ∗ T+.5)/100
```

Lines 4120 to 4160 give the computer operator the choice of returning to the beginning of the display function or ending the program. This feature can be used, for example, at the end of the year when the program is first run to determine the totals for the last quarter. The program could then be returned to the beginning of the display routine to total and display the amounts for the entire year.

Step 21.   Type In and Enter:

```
4120 PRINT:Y=1:N=2: INPUT"RETURN TO DISPLAY/TOTAL ROUTINE (Y/N)
";Y
4130 ON Y GOTO 3000, 4160
4150 GOTO 4120
4160 PRINT "THE END":END
```

LEVEL II - The same substitution for the Yes/No routine must be made. This substitution was originally described on page 51.

Level II Substitution

```
4120 PRINT:INPUT"RETURN TO DISPLAY/TOTAL ROUTINE (Y/N)"; Y$
4130 IF Y$="Y" THEN 3000
4140 IF Y$="N" THEN 4160
```

CREATING ORIGINAL PROGRAMS

The Payroll Program has shown how a computer can be used to achieve a specific job. This information provides the reader with a working knowledge of the programing process. The following section will describe how to use this knowledge to create original programs that can perform a multitude of different tasks.

The key to effective programing is to take the overall job that is to be done by the computer and break it down into its individual parts. This process takes the large number of choices that will be made in creating a program and narrows the focus down to the one or two choices that must be made to form the individual parts of the larger program. Once these smaller tasks have been identified, they may be translated into computer language.

1. Is the Job Appropriate for a Computer?

The first decision to make in creating any program is whether or not a given job is appropriate for the computer. Two basic criteria are used here in making this decision.

The first criteria is that the job to be programed involves paperwork and/or mathematical calculations. Computers are particularly suitable for paperwork because the standard equipment that is currently available uses a Video Screen to display the information and printers to generate printed data. Devices which do manual chores are not as readily available at the time of this writing.

The second criteria is that the computer is being used as a time saving device. The guidelines which follow are not necessarily appropriate for people who are using computers for experimental purposes or as a hobby.

Based on these criteria, the following questions will help determine how useful the computer will be in executing a given job.

1. How often will the program be run?

It will take a minimum of four to six times as long to create a program as it takes to do that job one time without a computer. If the job is only done once a year, there may be no time saving benefit from creating a program to do the task.

2. Does the information being processed repeat a format?

If the information being processed is constantly changing, such as in writing personal letters, there is probably no point in running it through a computer. On the other hand, information that is repeated, such as in form letters, is probably worth processing through a computer program.

3. Can the information be initially entered into the computer?

If the information to be processed must be first written out in long hand or typed on a typewriter and then entered into the computer, the time saving factor is greatly reduced.

Take, for example, a personal checking account. The check may be initially written in a variety of different locations. The initial information is entered on the check and into the checkbook. If the information is later entered into the computer, this would be a further duplication and therefore not very efficient. On the other hand, for a payroll checking account, adding a printer and a print function to the Payroll Program will enable the computer to automatically produce the payroll checks. This is very efficient because the initial information used to determine the payroll checks was entered directly into the computer.

4. How complicated is the job?

The more complicated the job, the more time the computer will save. The computer can follow a vast array of instructions and perform complicated calculations almost instantaneously. In the Payroll Program, for example, the computer does all the payroll calculations in about as much time as it takes to type in the number of hours for the employees.

5. How frequently are the calculations repeated?

The more frequently a calculation is repeated, the more effective the computer will become in saving time. Once again, in the Payroll Program it takes almost the same time to write the program for 20 employees as it takes to write it for 1 employee.

6. How many different ways will the information be used?

The more different outputs that are required for a single job, the more effective the computer will be in saving time. This is the reason why computers are so valuable a tool for business. A simple transaction, such as the sale of a product or service, creates a mound of paperwork including sales slips, inventory records, purchase orders, ledger entries, profit and loss statements, sales tax records, income tax records, etc. All of these outputs may be generated from appropriate computer programs.

2. Describe the Job

Once it has been determined that a job is appropriate for programing, the job should be carefully described. Write down the job description as clearly, logically, and completely as possible. The following questions should be considered.

1. What is the main objective of the job?

Programing will be a lot easier if the computer is asked to achieve one specific task in any given program. The general nature of this job should be described in a word or two. For the Payroll Program, the job is to calculate the payroll.

2. What fixed information will the program need?

The beginning of any program is the information that is required to achieve the designated job. This information will vary little, if at all, from one run of the program to the next. It will be included as a part of the program so that it does not have to be typed in each time. In the Payroll Program, this information includes the tax tables for the withholding information and the employees' data files.

Include only information that is essential to the operation of the program. For example, if the Payroll Totaling Program is going to be used to print W-2 forms, the full name and the Social Security number of each employee would have to be stored in the program. If this program is not going to print these forms, this information does not need to be included.

3. What information will be added during the run?

Information that changes from one run of the program to the next is entered into the program through INPUT Instructions. This information is normally created by the transaction which generates the job the computer is being programed to do. For example, the Payroll Program is created because the employees have worked a certain number of hours for which they wish to be paid. These hours are the Input information.

4. What calculations are performed with the information?

This is the middle of the job. Once the computer has been given all of the information, it must do something with this data. The calculations may simply be adding the information together to arrive at a total or they may involve an incredibly complicated series of computations.

5. What kind of output is required to complete the job?

This is the end of the job. It is during this part of the program that the results of the job are produced. There are three basic types of output that are most commonly created by a program. The resulting information may be displayed on the Video Screen, printed on a printer, or stored on a magnetic recording device. A program may have several different formats for the information with any one of these outputs depending on the specific requirements of the job being performed. For example, in the Payroll Program the information was displayed on the Video Screen in three different tables to show the employee data files, the employees' time and gross pay, and the final payroll information.

3. Assign Line Numbers

The final aspect in planning a program is to assign groups of Line Numbers to each of the functions the program is going to perform. The following breakdown is a suggestion only. It may be modified to suit the needs and desires of the individual programer.

Line Numbers	Function
$\emptyset\emptyset\emptyset$ to 999	Information and Program Control
1$\emptyset\emptyset\emptyset$ to 1999	Calculations
2$\emptyset\emptyset\emptyset$ to 2999	Display of Information and Calculations
3$\emptyset\emptyset\emptyset$ to 3999	Corrections
4$\emptyset\emptyset\emptyset$ on	Program Outputs in Required Formats

Program Information

The first step in writing a program is to make provisions for the information that is required to accomplish the task. Fixed information will be written into the program. Input information will be provided for by creating INPUT Instructions.

1. Stored Infomation

Fixed information is stored in a program so that it will not have to be typed in each time the program is run. This may be done in one of two ways. The information may be written directly into program lines or it may be stored in DATA Instructions and retrieved by READ Instructions. The choice of which to use will depend primarily on the permanence of the information.

Information is written directly into program lines when it is fairly permanent in nature. In the Payroll Program, the tax tables are written directly into the program lines because they will only be changed once a year.

Information is also written directly into program lines when it is only going to be used once during the program.

Normally, this type of information falls logically into place as the program develops. There is no need to preplan where it should be located in the program.

Information that may or may not change from one run of the program to the next can be introduced through DATA Instructions. It is also advisable to put information in DATA Lines when the same information will be used in different locations within the program.

In the Payroll Program, the employee records were kept in DATA Instructions. In other programs, DATA Instructions could be used to store the names and addresses of regular customers, product suppliers, etc. They could also be used to store information about products or services that are sold by a given business.

Some programs may not need any DATA Instructions.

It is very important to carefully preplan the nature of this information so that all possible uses are taken into consideration. For example, one function of the program might use one part of the information from a DATA Instruction. A later function might need different information. If all the uses for the information are not preplanned, the READ and DATA Instructions may have to be rewritten several times. For example, in the Payroll Program the names of the employees were used in the initial program lines.

The Marital Status and Tax Exemptions were not used until the calculation section.

A good way to plan DATA Instructions is to write out the data in a table. An example of this is the table for the Employee Records shown on page 37.

Each DATA Instruction should start out with a number, such as the Employee Number, which will label the information in the rest of that particular data line. Indicate this number in the first column of the table.

At the bottom of the table, a sample READ Instruction may be written to indicate the Variables that are assigned to recover the information from the DATA Instructions. The specific name of the Variable can be any letter of the alphabet (or other valid name) that makes sense to the programer. The Variables used in the READ Instructions should also be recorded on a separate piece of paper so that they will not be duplicated later when another part of the program is being written. Appendix B is a chart of the Variables and the Arrays that are used in the Payroll Program and the Payroll Totaling Program.

After the data has been planned out and written into the table, it may then be entered into the computer as program lines. The block of Line Numbers from 5ØØ to 999 may be reserved for DATA Instructions. This set of Line Numbers should also contain REM Instructions which clearly identify the information in the DATA Instructions. DATA Instructions were described on page 37. The REM Instructions which accompany them are described on page 42.

2. Input Information

All information that varies from one run of the program to the next is entered into the program through INPUT Instructions. This information is stored in the program either in Variables or Arrays.

Variables are used to store single pieces of information such as the date the program is being run. If a given Variable is used in more than one INPUT Instruction, the computer will only remember the last peice of data that is entered.

Arrays are used when a given format of information is to be repeated for a series of transactions. The specific names of the Variables within the Array are changed as the program progresses from one transaction to the next.

Radio Shack's Level I has only one Array, A( ). This Array may be used for different information within a given transaction by assigning blocks of numbers within the Array name to different types of data, such as A(I), A(I+5Ø), A(I+1ØØ), etc.

Level II has a considerable advantage over Level I because instead of one Array name, there are many. The Array name may be any single letter of the alphabet, A( ) to Z( ); any combination of two letters of the alphabet, AA( ) to ZZ( ); or any combination of a single letter followed by a single numeral, AØ( ) to Z9( ). These Arrays in Level II may be either Numeric Arrays or String Arrays. The String Arrays are created by adding a dollar sign at the end of the Array name, A$( ). This makes Level II considerably more flexible than Level I. In the rest of this section, suggested Array names for Level II will be indicated in boxes with double ruled lines. For Array names of other computer models, check the the owner's manual.

Input information should be carefully considered so that the essential information is included in the program and unnecessary information is left out. Take, for example, the transfer of a product to a customer who is to be billed for it at a later date. It is obviously necessary to identify who the customer is in the records the program maintains. If the computer is used with a printer, this information can include the customer's full name and billing address so that the computer can generate both a sales receipt and the billing statement. On the other hand, if there is no printer, there is no point in entering anything other than the customer's last name and maybe an initial. The rest of the information would be kept on a hand written sales receipt and later transferred to a typed billing. Entering the information a third time into the computer is a waste of time.

INPUT Instructions should include a label that will print on the Video Screen the name of the information that is being requested by the program. This label is created by putting a print statement inside quotation marks immediately after the INPUT Instruction. For example, 5∅ INPUT"THE DATE IS"; D. INPUT Instructions were described on pages 24 to 26.

3. Processing Information

A program must receive information before that information can be processed. For this reason, the INPUT Instructions are located in the program as the first group of Line Numbers.

Before the INPUT Instructions can be processed, however, the very first Line Numbers must clear any stray information out of the Arrays and Variables. This is particularly important when an Array or Variable may appear in a display routine or totaling function before it is processed through an INPUT Instruction (see page 96). In Level I, Arrays and Variables are cleared by typing in each Variable name and setting its value at zero, A(1)=∅.

In Level II the Arrays and Variables are cleared by typing the instruction CLEAR into an early Line Number, 1∅ CLEAR. This instruction automatically sets all Arrays and Variables at zero.

During these intial lines, the Dimension of Level II Arrays must be established. First, determine the maximum number of transactions a program will process, then write appropriate DIM Instructions, 2∅ DIM A(5∅), A1(5∅), A2(5∅), etc. The DIM Instruction must include the names of all Arrays that are to be used in the program. DIM Instructions were described on page 45.

After these initial lines have been written, the INPUT Instructions may be typed into the program. The first INPUT Instructions are used to label the specific run of the program that is being processed. The information in the label will not be repeated in the program so it may be stored in a Variable.

```
50 INPUT "THE DATE IS"; D
```

After the program is labeled, the information for the body of the program may be established. The INPUT Instructions for this part of the program may be processed several different ways, depending on the nature of the task being performed. Read through this section carefully and determine the routines that will be required. Then write out all of the computer instructions that are to be used on a piece of scratch paper. Make sure these instructions follow the correct sequence. Then go back and add Line Numbers to the instructions. Finally, type this part of the program into the computer.

The information that is the basis for the program is frequently derived from a series of transactions. The information from these transactions is stored in Arrays. The INPUT Instructions for the Arrays must be put inside a program loop that will change the name of the Variables in the Array for each subsequent transaction.

There are two types of loops that may be used for these Arrays. The first loop is used when there are a known number of transactions to be recorded. The second loop is used when the specific number of transactions to be processed is not known at the time the program is started.

When a specified number of transactions is to be entered into the program, a FOR NEXT Loop is used to repeat the INPUT Instructions. Upon completion of the designated number of passes, the computer will proceed with the rest of the program. An example of this type of loop is shown below. The FOR NEXT Loop was described on page 29. Its use in the Payroll Program was described on pages 39 and 40.

```
60 INPUT "NUMBER OF TRANSACTIONS"; N
70 FOR I = 1 TO N
260 INPUT "FIRST DATA"; A(I)
270 INPUT "SECOND DATA"; A(I + 50)    B(I)
290 NEXT I
```

The second type of loop will process an unspecified number of transactions. This type of loop uses a GOTO Instruction to repeat the INPUT Instructions. A special code for the first INPUT Instruction will break the loop. This code should be a piece of data that would not normally be entered as a result of a regular transaction. An IF THEN Instruction tests the information from the first INPUT Instruction to see if the code has been used. If the code is not used, the loop continues to function. If the code is used, the program is directed to a program line that is past the loop. This type of GOTO Loop was described on pages 27 and 28.

```
60 I = 0
70 I = I + 1
250 INPUT"FIRST DATA (-99 TO CONTINUE PROGRAM)"; A(I)
260 IF A(I) = -99 THEN 290
270 INPUT "SECOND DATA"; A(I + 50)        B(I)
290 GOTO 70
295 N = I
```

Notice in this routine a counting device, the Variable I, is used to change the name of the Array. Each time the loop makes another pass, the value of I is increased by one (Line 70). The total number of loops the program makes is recorded in the Variable N (Line 295). This value may be used later in the program in a FOR NEXT Loop to display all of the information that has been put into the program.

4. Correlating INPUT and DATA Information

In some programs, it may be necessary to correlate the information from the DATA Instructions with the information that is to be entered in the INPUT Instructions. In the Payroll Program this was easy to do because all of the data files were used. The program read each data file, printed the name from a given file, and asked for the corresponding Input information (pages 43 and 44). A similar routine is shown below.

```
10 N = 3
70 FOR I = 1 TO N
150 READ C,A$,Z              C(I), A$(I), Z(I)
250 PRINT"DATA FOR"; A$      A$(I)
260 INPUT"FIRST DATA"; A(I + 50)     A1(I)
270 INPUT"SECOND DATA"; A(I + 100)   A2(I)
290 NEXT I
```

Certain programs will need the information from only one or two of many data files. For example, if the data files contain customer information, not every customer is going to buy something every day. If this is the case, the following routine may be added to the instructions on the previous page. This routine pulls one particular file. The Array A(I) remembers the number of the file that is pulled for a given transaction. The Variable F records the total number of files in the DATA Instructions in this example. This same routine was used in the Payroll Program for expanding the Correction Subroutine (pages 60 to 62).

```
10 F = 20
60 INPUT"NUMBER OF TRANSACTIONS"; N
150 RESTORE:INPUT"PULL DATA FILE #"; A(I)
160 FOR X = 1 TO F
170 READ C,A$,Z                    C,A$(I),Z(I)
180 IF C = A(I) THEN 250
190 NEXT X
200 GOTO 150
```

If there are a great number of data files, a separate written record of the data files' numbers and names may be kept near the computer. This written record may be used to select the number of the file desired. This approach is faster and more efficient than displaying a large number of files on the screen every time a new transaction is processed.

If there are only a few data files, the following routine can print all of the numbers and names of each data file so that the computer operator will know which file number to select.

The semi-colon at the end of Line 130 signals the computer to print each number and name, one right after the other.

```
110 FOR X = 1 TO F
120 READ C,A$,Z
130 PRINT " #";C;" NAME";A$;
140 NEXT X
```

Level II has a feature that can be used to select the appropriate data files if names are used. This routine will compare one String Variable with another String Variable and if the two match, letter for letter, the computer's brain will realize they are the same. The spelling must be exactly the same in both Variables including the use of the Shift Key. Lines 15Ø and 18Ø from above have to be rewritten to use this feature.

```
150 RESTORE: INPUT"PULL DATA FILE FOR"; P$(I)
180 IF A$(I) = P$(I) THEN 250
```

Another feature of Level II is that its extended Array capability allows a program to select either information from a DATA Instruction or information that is not stored in a program. For example, this could be used in the Payroll Program for part-time help that works during one pay period. The information about the part-time employees' withholding exemptions, etc. could be entered into the program through INPUT Instructions.

Lines 8Ø and 9Ø allow the computer operator to select information either from DATA Instructions or INPUT Instructions. Lines 21Ø to 23Ø are the INPUT Instructions for the new data.

```
80 INPUT"INPUT FOR: 1. STORED NAME, 2. NEW
NAME"; A
90 ON A GOTO 110, 210
100 GOTO 80
210 INPUT "#"; A(I)
220 INPUT"NAME"; A$(I)
230 INPUT"ZIP"; Z(I)
```

Program Calculations

Once the information is entered into the program, the computer must be instructed to manipulate this data to produce the information required to complete the job. This is the heart of the program. In the Payroll Program, this is the section that calculates the employees' pay and deductions.

There are an infinite variety of ways a computer can manipulate information with varying degrees of complexity, depending on the nature of the job being performed. However, the basis for all of these manipulations is six computer instructions: FOR NEXT, IF THEN, GOTO, GOSUB, ON GOTO, and ON GOSUB. To determine when to use the appropriate instruction, first write out the task to be performed in terms a human being can understand.

The best way to write out a job description for the program is to do the job once, very carefully. At each step, write out very precise instructions describing what must be done. Describe the task as if it were to be done by a very dumb, very literal person who has never done anything like it before. The description should be so clear, concise, precise and complete that if it is followed exactly, it would be impossible to do the job wrong.

For the Payroll Program, the description of the calculations may be written as indicated below. The translations into computer language occur on the pages indicated in parentheses.

1. Calculate the Gross Pay by adding the employee's hours for both weeks together and multiplying this by the hourly pay (page 54).

2. Determine overtime pay for any week with more than 40 hours. Subtract 40 from the total hours for this week and multiply the result by half the hourly pay rate. Add this to the Gross Pay (page 73).

3. Calculate the State Disability Insurance by multiplying the Gross Pay by 1% (page 74).

4. Calculate the Social Security Tax for any employee whose annual wages are less than $22,900 at 6.13% of the Gross Pay (page 75).

5. Determine the Federal Income Tax by following the steps in the Federal Employer's Tax Guide (pages 77 to 79).

6. Determine the State Income Tax by following the steps in the State Employer's Tax Guide (pages 79 to 86).

7. Calculate the Net Pay by subtracting the Federal Income Tax, Social Security, State Income Tax and State Disability Insurance from the Gross Pay (page 86).

Once the job has been described in this manner, it may be translated into computer terms. The six basic computer instructions and their respective translations are listed below.

FOR NEXT - Repeat this series of instructions for the designated number of times.

IF THEN - Compare these two values and determine whether the value to the left is equal to (=), greater than (>), or lesser than (<) the value to the right.

GOTO - At this point, go to the designated step.

GOSUB - Go to the designated series of instructions and upon completion, come back to this point in the instructions.

ON GOTO - Go to one of the designated instructions based on the information received prior to this point and continue from there. there.

ON GOSUB - Go to one of the designated series of instructions based on the information received up to this point and return here upon completion of those instructions.

Based on these six instructions there are many different directions the program can follow. The success of these program manipulations and their accompanying calculations can be judged by whether or not the program produces the correct results.

The program manipulations and their accompanying calculations may be performed either after each transaction has been entered into the computer or after all of the information has been typed in.

To have the calculations performed at the end of each transaction, put a GOSUB Instruction after the last INPUT Instruction of the transaction and before the NEXT (or GOTO) Instruction which starts the program on the next transaction. A RETURN Instruction must be placed at the end of the calculation/manipulation routine.

```
285 GOSUB 1000
1990 RETURN
```

If the calculations are to be performed after all the transactions have been entered, the GOSUB Instruction will have to come after the NEXT Instruction which processes the transaction. A FOR NEXT Loop will have to be placed around the manipulation/calculation routine so that all the transactions will be processed.

```
310 GOSUB 1000
1000 FOR I = 1 TO N
1980 NEXT I
1990 RETURN
```

Program Outputs

After all of the information has been manipulated to produce the results desired, these results must be displayed in some manner so that the information may be used.

Most micro-computers are designed to display the information on a Video Screen, print it on a printer, and store the data on a magnetic recording device. These basic functions may be used to display the information in a wide variety of formats, but each type of function follows a definite sequence of computer instructions. The sequence for each of the outputs will be described in this section. First, however, it is necessary to create a routine that will select the appropriate function that the computer operator wants the program to execute.

1. Program Control

The Program Control is a series of PRINT Instructions which lists all of the possible computer functions the operator may choose from. Each function is assigned a number. An INPUT Instruction allows the operator to enter the appropriate selection. An ON GOSUB Instruction then directs the program to the function desired. This routine was described for the Payroll Program on pages 57 to 59.

```
300 CLS: PRINT"DISPLAY CONTENTS (1)"
310 PRINT"ADDITIONAL CORRECTIONS (2)"
320 PRINT"STORE INFORMATION (3)"
330 PRINT"RETRIEVE INFORMATION (4)"
340 PRINT"PRINT INFORMATION (5)"
350 PRINT"END PROGRAM (6)"
360 INPUT A
370 ON A GOSUB 2000, 3000, 4000, 5000, 6000
380 IF A = 6 THEN 400
390 GOTO 300
400 END
```

2. Video Displays

Video Displays are created by using PRINT and TAB Instructions to present the information stored in Variables and Arrays in some meaningful format.

Appendix C is a Video Display worksheet which may be duplicated by the reader and used to predetermine the format for the displays desired.

Below is a basic display routine with the instructions listed in the appropriate sequence. The chart to the left of the program lines indicates the four basic parts of the display routine. "Head" is the part of the program which prints the headings for the information in the table. "Info" prints the data stored in the Arrays. "Total" adds the information from the Arrays for each transaction to derive a total for all the information. "Stop" is the routine which stops the program after ten lines of information have been displayed. The basic display routine for the Payroll Program was described on pages 38 to 40. Totaling was described on page 56. The "Stop" function was described on pages 93 and 94.

HEAD	INFO	TOTAL	STOP	
		X		2000 T = 0 : U = 0
			X	2010 S = 1
X				2020 CLS : PRINT TAB(28); "HEADING"
X				2030 PRINT : PRINT"#"; TAB(5); "DATA 1"; TAB(15);"DATA 2"
		X		2040 FOR I = 1 TO N
	X			2050 PRINT A(I); TAB(4); A(50 + I); TAB(14); A(100 + I)
		X		2060 T = T + A(50 + I) : U = U + A(100 + I)
			X	2070 S = S + 1
			X	2080 IF S = 10 THEN 2100
			X	2090 GOTO 2130
			X	2100 S = 1 : INPUT"CONTINUE"; A
X			X	2110 CLS : PRINT TAB(28); "HEADING"
X			X	2120 PRINT : PRINT"#"; TAB(5); "DATA 1"; TAB(15); "DATA 2"
		X		2130 NEXT I
		X		2140 PRINT"——————————————————————————"
		X		2150 PRINT TAB(4); T; TAB(14); U
				2160 INPUT"CONTINUE"; Y
				2170 RETURN

DATA 1 = A1(I)
DATA 2 = A2(I)

3. Correction Routine

As the information is being displayed, an incorrect entry may be discovered. A correction routine will be required to change the error.

The basic correction routine will consist of four parts. The first part will allow the computer operator to "Pull" the incorrect transaction from the computer's memory. "Select" allows the operator to select the Array that is to be changed. "Correct" places the Array with the error back into an INPUT Instruction so the correct data may be entered. "Next" allows the computer operator to choose between correcting another transaction, the same transaction, or to continue with the rest of the program.

PULL	SELECT	CORRECT	NEXT	
X				3000 CLS:INPUT"CORRECT TRANSACTION #"; I
	X			3010 INPUT"CORRECT: 1.FIRST DATA, 2.SECOND DATA";Y
	X			3020 ON Y GOTO 3040, 3060
	X			3030 GOTO 3010
		X		3040 INPUT"FIRST DATA"; A(50 + I)
		X		3050 GOTO 3070
		X		3060 INPUT"SECOND DATA"; A(100 + I)
		X		3070 GOSUB 1000 : REM - CALCULATIONS
			X	3080 PRINT"CORRECT: 1.ANOTHER TRANSACTION, ";
			X	3081 INPUT"2.SAME , 3.CONTINUE PROGRAM"; A
			X	3090 ON A GOTO 3000, 3010, 3110
			X	3100 GOTO 3080
				3110 RETURN

A1(I)

A2(I)

If the Correction Routine is going to be used to change information as it is initially entered into the program, the following lines must be added to the first part of the program. Notice that the GOSUB Instruction bypasses the "Pull" function. The transaction to be corrected does not have to be Pulled from the computer's memory because it is the transaction that is currently being processed.

```
280 Y = 1: N = 2: INPUT"CORRECTIONS (Y/N)"; A
281 ON A GOTO 284, 290
283 GOTO 280
284 GOSUB 3010
```

Level II Substitution

```
280 INPUT"CORRECTIONS (Y/N)"; Y$
281 IF Y$ = "Y" THEN 284
282 IF Y$ = "N" THEN 290
```

4. Storing and Retrieving Data

The computer function that retrieves information stored on a cassette tape is almost identical to the function that records the information in the first place. Both functions require several program lines which "Alert" the computer operator to prepare and turn off the tape recorder. The specific program lines which "Store" the information must have the same sequence of data as the program lines which "Retrieve" that information. The only difference between the two functions is that the Retrieval Function has a "Select" routine which allows the computer operator the opportunity to make sure that the information desired is being retrieved from the correct location on the tape. These functions were described for the Payroll Program on pages 65 to 70.

ALERT	STORE	RETRIEVE	SELECT	
X				4000 PRINT"PREPARE TO RECORD INFORMATION"
X				4010 INPUT"IS THE TAPE RECORDER IN RECORD (Y)";A
	X			4020 PRINT#D;",";N
	X			4030 FOR I = 1 TO N
	X			4040 PRINT#A(I);",";A(I + 50);",";A(I + 100)
	X			4050 NEXT I
X				4060 PRINT"THE INFORMATION IS RECORDED"
X				4070 INPUT"TURN OFF THE TAPE RECORDER (Y)";A
				4080 RETURN
X				5000 PRINT"PREPARE TO RETRIEVE INFORMATION"
X				5010 INPUT"IS THE TAPE RECORDER IN PLAY (Y)";A
		X		5020 INPUT#D,N
			X	5030 PRINT"THIS DATE IS"; D
			X	5040 INPUT"RETRIEVE: 1.THIS DATE, 2.ANOTHER";A
			X	5050 ON A GOTO 5070, 5010
			X	5060 GOTO 5040
		X		5070 FOR I = 1 TO N
		X		5080 INPUT#A(I),A(I + 50),A(I + 100)
		X		5090 NEXT I
X				5100 PRINT"THE INFORMATION IS RETRIEVED"
X				5110 INPUT"TURN OFF THE TAPE RECORDER (Y)";A
				5120 RETURN

Level II Substitution

```
4020 PRINT#−1,D,N
4040 PRINT#−1,A(I),A1(I),A2(I)
5020 INPUT#−1, D, N
5080 INPUT#−1, A(I), A1(I), A2(I)
```

5. Printing Information

Radio Shack's Level I cannot be used with a printer.   However, Level II and many other computer models can be.   The specific computer instructions that may be used with a printer will vary according to the specifications of the equipment.   The basic format for the Print Function will include "Alert" Instructions to tell the computer operator to make sure the equipment is ready and the paper is in place in the printer.   Then a series of instructions such as LPRINT are used to activate the printer.

ALERT	PRINT	
X		6000 INPUT"IS THE PRINTER READY";Y
X		6010 LPRINT"THE DATE IS";D
	X	6020 LPRINT:LPRINT"HEADING"
	X	6030 LPRINT"#","DATA 1", "DATA 2"
	X	6040 FOR I=1 TO N
	X	6050 LPRINT A(I), A1(I), A2(I)
	X	6060 NEXT I
X		6070 PRINT"THE INFORMATION IS PRINTED"
X		6080 INPUT"CONTINUE THE PROGRAM";A
		6090 RETURN

Debugging Programs

Computers are very precise creatures, far more so than human beings. For example, Hi and Hello mean the same thing to people unless they are told otherwise. Hi and Hello have two completely different meanings to the computer unless it is told otherwise.

This difference in thinking styles may lead to a few problems when original programs are created. These problems will become less frequent as the programer learns to think more like a computer.

The process of correcting problems so that programs run correctly is called Debugging. There are essentially two types of bugs that creep into programs, typographical errors and programing errors.

A typographical error in a Line Number can cause real problems because it can put the instruction in the wrong part of the program. For example, Line 3ØØ will not work very well if it is entered as Line 3Ø. It will also drop the instructions which were in Line 3Ø out of the computer's memory.

Typographical errors in instruction names or computer signals will create error messages. And typographical errors within instructions will generate incorrect results for the program.

Programing errors occur when an instruction is left out of a given routine such as leaving the NEXT out of a FOR NEXT Loop or a RETURN out of a GOSUB Instruction.

Another type of programing error occurs when the computer is not sent in the correct direction at some point in the program. For example, if the GOTO Instructions are left off the end of the instructions for the tax tables (see page 78), the computer will perform all of the calculations instead of just one calculation from the appropriate line.

The program format described in this book is designed to minimize the problems encountered in developing programs. First, individual parts of the program are tested out as they are entered into the computer. Secondly, the division of the program into separate functions makes it easier to locate the specific function that is creating the problem.

The first step in debugging a program is to analyze the specific nature of the error. Is the program not doing something it should be doing or is the information generated by the program incorrect?

Next, locate the source of the problem by determining which function or group of Line Numbers is generating the error. Continue to narrow down the problem until the specific line responsible is discovered.

A computer instruction which may help with this process is STOP. This instruction will Stop the run of the program at a specific Line Number. First, determine where the problem is probably occuring. Then type in a temporary Line Number and the instruction STOP. When the program is run, it will Stop at this line. The programer can then analyze what is happening.

During the STOP Instruction, the values in the Arrays may be examined by typing in PRINT A( ) with the Variable name being indicated between the parentheses. There is no Line Number for the PRINT Instruction so the information will be printed as soon as the Enter Key is pressed.

To examine more than one Variable in an Array, or several Arrays, type in a FOR NEXT Loop as shown below. The colons allow several instructions to be written in. Once again, the lack of a Line Number means this series of instructions will be executed as soon as the Enter Key is pressed.

FOR E = 1 to 10: PRINT E,A(E),A(E + 50): NEXT E

The value in a Variable may also be changed while the program is stopped, A(21)=$\emptyset$.

To continue the program after a STOP Instruction, type in CONT and press the Enter Key. Keep a record of the Line Numbers that are used for the STOP Instructions so that these instructions may be removed once the program is running properly.

The Break Key will stop the program also. The main advantage of the STOP Instruction over the Break Key is that the STOP Instruction may be placed at a specific point in the program.

Level II has another handy debugging instruction, TRON. This instruction makes the computer print every Line Number in the program that is processed during a given run. This instruction is used if the program is not following the correct series of instructions. TRON is typed in without a Line Number either before the run of a program is started, after a STOP Instruction, or after the Break Key is pressed. TRON is deactivated by typing in TROFF.

Appendix A – State Tax (Step 2)

Step 2 of the California Employer's Tax Guide allows employees to declare exemptions for itemized deductions. To include this in the Payroll Program, the READ and DATA Instructions must be expanded to include the additional data. The Variable Z is used in the READ Instructions to retrieve this new piece of data. The table which displays the Employee Records must be rewritten to include the new classification (Lines 7011, 7012, 7050, and 7051). Finally, three lines in the Calculation section have to be changed. Line 1330 directed the program from Step 1 of the State Tax calculations to Step 3. It must be rewritten to send the program to the new Step 2 routine. Lines 1410 and 1430 originally calculated the taxable income from the Gross Pay, A(E). They must now calculate the taxable income from the results of Step 2 as stored in the Variable S.

```
505 REM —5. NUMBER OF TAX EXEMPTIONS (X), 5A. SPECIAL (Z)
508 REM —000 DATA E, A$, H, M, X, Z, C
510 DATA 1, HARRISON, 3.25, 1, 1, 2, 1
520 DATA 2, SAMUELS, 3.50, 3, 4, 1, 1
530 DATA 3, JOHNSON, 4.75, 2, 2, 0, 1
110 READ E, A$, H, M, X, Z, C
910 READ E, A$, H, M, X, Z, C
2030 READ E, A$, H, M, X, Z, C
3020 READ E, A$, H, M, X, Z, C
3080 READ E, A$, H, M, X, Z, C
4040 READ E, A$, H, M, X, Z, C
7040 READ E, A$, H, M, X, Z, C
7011 PRINT TAB(28); "MAR STATUS"; TAB(41); "TAX EX"; TAB(50);
7012 PRINT "SP. EX"; TAB(58); "CODE"
7050 PRINT E; TAB(5); A$; TAB(19); H; TAB(31); M; TAB(42); X;
7051 PRINT TAB(51); Z; TAB(58); C
1330 GOTO 1360
1410 S=S—38.46:GOTO 1450
1430 S=S—76.92
```

TABLE B - Itemized Deduction Allowance Table

Additional withholding allowances+	Payroll period							
	Weekly	Biweekly	Semimonthly	Monthly	Quarterly	Semiannual	Annual	Daily or miscellaneous
1	$14	$29	$31	$63	$188	$375	$750	$2.00
2	29	58	63	125	375	750	1,500	4.00
3	43	87	94	188	563	1,125	2,250	6.00
4	58	115	125	250	750	1,500	3,000	8.00
5	72	144	156	313	938	1,875	3,750	10.00
6	87	173	188	375	1,125	2,250	4,500	12.00
7	101	202	219	438	1,313	2,625	5,250	14.00
8	115	231	250	500	1,500	3,000	6,000	16.00
9	130	260	281	563	1,688	3,375	6,750	18.00
10*	144	288	313	625	1,875	3,750	7,500	21.00

* If the number of additional withholding allowances for itemized deductions claimed is greater than 10, multiply the amount shown for one additional withholding allowance by the number claimed.

Table B determines how much money is subtracted from the Gross Pay, A(E), according to the number of special exemptions that are claimed by the employee, the Variable Z. The resulting taxable income is stored in the Variable S.

If no special allowances are claimed, Line 1360 sets the value of S at the Gross Pay. The program proceeds to Line 1400 which starts the calculations for the regular tax exemptions.

If one to ten special exemptions are claimed, Line 1370 counts over to the appropriate Line Number for the deduction.

If more than ten exemptions are claimed, Line 1380 directs the program to Line 1391 for the appropriate calculation.

```
1360 IF Z=0 THEN S=A(E):GOTO1400
1370 ON Z GOTO 1381, 1382, 1383, 1384, 1385, 1386, 1387, 1388, 1389, 1390
1380 GOTO 1391
1381 S=A(E)-29:GOTO 1400
1382 S=A(E)-58:GOTO 1400
1383 S=A(E)-87:GOTO 1400
1384 S=A(E)-115:GOTO 1400
1385 S=A(E)-144: GOTO 1400
1386 S=A(E)-173:GOTO 1400
1387 S=A(E)-202:GOTO 1400
1388 S=A(E)-231:GOTO 1400
1389 S=A(E)-260:GOTO 1400
1390 S=A(E)-288:GOTO 1400
1391 S=A(E)-Z * 29
```

Appendix B – Chart of Variables

	PAYROLL PROGRAM	PAYROLL TOTALING PROGRAM
A	Answers to INPUT Questions	Answers to INPUT Questions
A$	Employee's Name	Employee's Name
B	Beginning Date of Pay Period	Beginning Pay Period
C	Employee Code	
D	Ending Date of Pay Period	Display Counting Device
E	Employee Number	Employee Number by Pay Period
F	Taxable Income (FIT)	Net Pay
G	Employee Number Corrected	Employee Number for Totals
H	Hourly Pay	Totals of Net Pay
I	Variable of FOR NEXT Loop	
J		Variable of FOR NEXT Loop
K		Number of Pay Periods Retrieved
L	Totals for SDI	Totals for SDI
M	Marital Status	
N	No Answer (N equals 2)	
O		
P	Totals for SIT	Totals for SIT
Q		
R		
S	Taxable Income (SIT)	
T	Totals for Gross Pay	Totals for Gross Pay
U	Totals for FIT	Totals for FIT
V	Totals for FICA	Totals for FICA
W	Number of Workers	Number of Workers
X	Tax Exemptions	
Y	Yes Answer (Y equals 1)	
Z	Special Exemptions for SIT	
A(E)	Gross Pay	Gross Pay
A(20+E)	Week 1 Hours	Federal Income Tax (FIT)
A(40+E)	Week 2 Hours	Social Security Tax (FICA)
A(60+E)	Social Security Tax (FICA)	State Income Tax (SIT)
A(80+E)	Federal Income Tax (FIT)	State Disability Insurance (SDI)
A(100+E)	State Income Tax (SIT)	
A(120+E)	State Disability Ins. (SDI)	
A(140+E)	Net Pay	

Appendix C – Video Display Worksheet

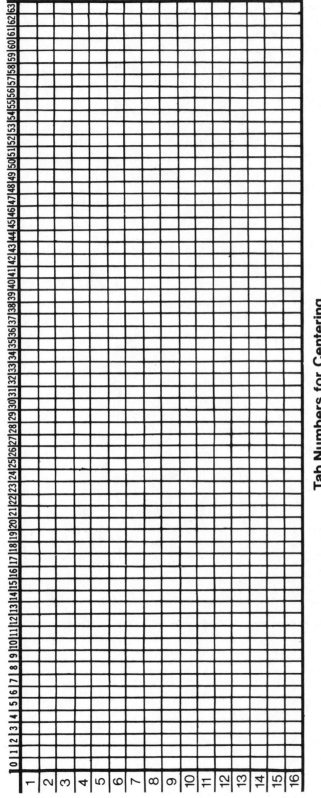

Tab Numbers for Centering

The exact Tab Number that is required to center a heading may be determined by using the chart above. Start at the left edge of this chart and write out the heading word for word and space for space as it is to appear. From the last letter or symbol on the right side of the line, go straight up to the tab number at the top of the chart. For example, the word HELLO may be centered on the screen by using TAB(29).

Index

Accuracy, 14
Arrays, 43, 45, 87-88, 96, 104-106, 119

Back Space Key, 11, 22
Break Key, 27
Byte, 31

Calculations, 36, 54-56, 101, 110-111
Cassette Tapes, 30-32, 68, 87
Clear Key, 13
CLEAR, 105
CLOAD, 32
CLS, 23, 38
Colon, 18
Comma, 26
CONT, 119
Continuous Loop, 27, 107
Corrections, 11-12, 14, 22, 49-53, 60-62, 114-115
Counting Routines, 93, 107
CSAVE, 31

DATA, 37, 41, 90, 103-104
Debugging Programs, 118-119
Deleting Lines, 23
DIM, 45, 89, 105
Display Routines, 38-41, 46-48, 61, 72-73, 90-95, 96-98, 113

Employee Code, 35, 37, 45
END, 27, 52, 59
Enter Key, 12, 13, 20, 42
Error Messages, 12, 14, 17

Federal Income Tax, 76-79
FOR NEXT, 29, 39-40, 62, 92, 95, 106-108, 111, 119

GOSUB, 51-53, 54-55, 111
GOTO, 27, 78, 107
Greater Than, 73
Gross Pay, 54, 56

IF THEN, 28, 73-74, 77-78, 107-109
INPUT, 24-26, 44, 49, 105-106
INPUT #, 68
Input Information, 36, 43-48, 101, 104-105
INT, 74

Less Than, 77
LET, 18
Line Numbers, 20, 23, 30, 33, 102, 106
LIST, 24, 31, 40
Loops, 27-29, 39-40, 62, 89-90, 92-93, 106-109

Math Functions, 16-17
Marital Status, 37
Memory, 18, 30-32, 33

Net Pay, 86, 91
NEW, 21, 31
Numeric Values, 15
Numeric Variables, 18

ON GOSUB, 58-59, 112
ON GOTO, 49-50, 77, 85
Overtime, 73-74

Parenthesis,
Parentheses, 16-17, 54
Pause Control, 47, 60, 93-94
PRINT, 12-13, 25, 38-39
PRINT #, 65-66
PRINT MEM, 31, 32
Printing Information, 117
Program Control, 57-58, 112
Program Lines, 20
Program Output, 36, 57-58, 102, 112-117
Program Sophistication, 63-64
Prompt Cursor, 11

Quotation Marks, 13, 15, 18

READ, 38, 104
REM, 42, 73
RESTORE, 40
Retrieving Information, 68-70, 86,
    88-90, 116
Retrieving Programs, 32
RETURN, 52
Rounding Off, 74
RUN, 21, 61

Semi-Colon, 15, 39, 108
Social Security Tax, 75
Spacing, 15, 33
State Disability Insurance, 74
State Income Tax, 79-86
STEP, 92
STOP, 119
Stored Information, 35, 37-42, 101,
    103-104
Storing Information, 65-68, 86, 116
Storing Programs, 32
String Variables, 18, 51, 109
Subroutines, 51-53, 54-55, 58-59,
    111

TAB, 38-39
Totaling Routines, 56, 95-96
TROFF, 119
TRON, 119

Variables, 18-19, 24-26, 30, 38, 43,
    56, 64, 104, 119

Yes/No Routines, 50-51, 52, 75, 98

Glossary

Arrays - Variables that can hold a vast "array" of information because the name of the Variable within an Array is established by a numeric value placed between the parentheses, A( ).

CLEAR - A Level II Instruction which clears the information out of Variables and Arrays.

CLOAD - Loads programs from cassette tapes into the computer.

CLS - Clears the Video Screen.

Colon - Separates two or more instructions in one program line.

Comma - Separates information in instructions.

CONT - Continues the program after a STOP Instruction or after the Break Key has been pressed.

DATA - Stores fixed information in a program.

DIM - A Level II Instruction which sets the number of Variables that are to be used in a given Array.

CSAVE - Saves programs on cassette tapes.   (Level II uses CSAVE "S".)

END - Ends the run of a program.

FOR NEXT - Repeats a series of instructions for a given number of times.

GOSUB - Directs the program to a specific series of instructions and has it return upon completion.

GOTO - Directs the program to a specific Line Number.

IF THEN - Tests the values in the first part of the instruction and either changes the program direction or establishes new values on the basis of the results.

INPUT - Accepts information into a Variable or Array during a program.

INPUT # - Retrieves information from tapes. (Level II uses INPUT #-1)

INT - Drops numeric values to the right of the decimal point.

LET - Establishes the value of a Variable.   The word let is optional, A=5.

LIST - Displays the instructions in a program.

NEW - Clears a program out of the computer's memory.

ON GOSUB - Directs the program to one of several subroutines based on the value in a Variable.

ON GOTO - Directs the program to one of several Line Numbers based on the value in a Variable.

Parentheses - Used to establish the sequence of mathematical calculations.

PRINT - Prints information on the Video Screen.

PRINT # - Stores information on cassette tape. (Level II uses PRINT #-1).

PRINT MEM - Prints the amount of unused memory.

Quotation Marks - Establishes the string of characters that are to be printed by the computer.

RUN - Starts the execution of a program.

Semi-Colon - Separates different information in PRINT Instructions

STEP - Sets the counting interval of FOR NEXT Loops.

STOP - Stops the run of a program.

TAB - Tells the computer where to start printing information in PRINT Lines.

TRON - Turns on a trace that prints the Line Numbers a program follows.

TROFF - Turns off the trace.   These instructions are for Level II computers.

Variables - Store information in a program.   Numeric Variables store numbers and String Variables store strings of characters.

Other Books from Design Enterprises

An Illustrated History of the Chinese in America
by Ruthanne Lum McCunn

With the current interest in China, this dramatic account of the Chinese in America serves as a timely eye opener to an untold chapter in American history.

Who flew the first aircraft on the West Coast? Who created the Star Trek monsters? Why are paper rings put around cigars? What was "The Island" and why was it dreaded? Why did the Chinese come? Why did they stay?

This lavishly illustrated work gives the answers to these questions and much more.

"Timely, instructive, and absorbing are adjectives earned by McCunn's account of Chinese immigrants in the U.S., a big book with maps and period photos (some reproduced here for the first time)."
Publishers Weekly

"... the best history book on Chinese Americans to come out so far."
East/West
The Chinese American Journal

How to Make Sewing Patterns
by Donald H. McCunn

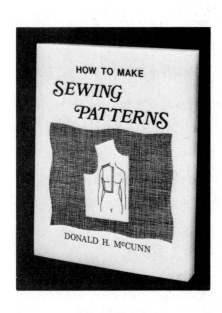

Learn how to make fitted patterns that show the shape of the body. Then see how these patterns may be changed to copy the latest styles, alter commercial patterns, and create original designs.

"How to Make Sewing Patterns is terrific - though I'm an excellent seamstress with 25 years experience, this book doubled my knowledge in one weeks time."
Judy Hopkins
Anchorage, Alaska

"McCunn's book dispels the mysteries of pattern drafting."
Library Journal

"The most readable pattern drafting book I've found."
Whole Earth Catalog (Epilog)

DESIGN ENTERPRISES OF SAN FRANCISCO
P.O. Box 27677
San Francisco, California, 94127

MAILING LIST

Please place me on your mailing list for future releases in the areas indicated below:

__ Computer Programing. Type of Computer: _____

Type of Applications: _____

__ Asian Studies

__ Fashion Design

Name: _____

Address: _____

_____ Zip: _____

ORDER FORM

Please send:

____ copies of "How to Make Sewing Patterns" @ $7.95

____ copies of "An Illustrated History of the Chinese in America"
(Hardback) @ $11.95

____ copies of "An Illustrated History of the Chinese in America"
(Paperback) @ $6.95

____ copies of "Computer Programing for the Complete Idiot" @ $5.95

Add $1.00 for shipping and handling. (Calif. residents add 6% sales tax.)

I have enclosed a check/money order for $_____.

Charge to my: __ Masguercharge, __ Visa.

Card #: _____ Expires: _____.

Name: _____

Address: _____

_____ Zip: _____